The Wisdo

For Sophie, James and Astrid

The Wisdom of the Heart

Dennis Lennon

First published in Great Britain in 2004 by
Society for Promoting Christian Knowledge
Holy Trinity Church
Marylebone Road
London NW1 4DU

British Library Cataloguing-in-Publication Data

A catalogue record for this book is available from the British Library

ISBN 0-281-05625-0

1 3 5 7 9 10 8 6 4 2

Typeset by Avocet Typeset, Chilton, Aylesbury, Bucks
Printed in Great Britain by Bookmarque Ltd, Croydon, Surrey

Contents

CHAPTER 1

Sophia's Children

Is it going too far to say that society is having a major attack of the sulks over Jesus? Some observers of the way we are today believe it doesn't go nearly far enough. They hold that a positive hatred for God has been a shaping and driving force in our civilization for the past 200 years. Evidently we are reaping the consequences. In an intriguing parable with a terrific sting in its tail, Jesus diagnosed people's attitude towards him as something simpler than hatred; more a childish peevishness:

> To what, then, can I compare the people of this generation? What are they like? They are like children sitting in the market-place and calling out to each other:
>
> 'We played the flute for you,
> and you did not dance;
> we sang a dirge,
> and you did not cry.'
>
> For John the Baptist came neither eating bread nor drinking wine, and you say, 'He has a demon.' The Son of Man came eating and drinking, and you say, 'He is a glutton and a drunkard, a friend of tax collectors and "sinners".' But wisdom is proved right by all her children.
>
> (Luke 7.31–35)

One hot afternoon, tired children bicker over which game to play next. Keep your eye on the boy with the flute and his pal with the drum, for they call the tunes – if only their friends will cooperate and follow their lead. 'Let's put on a wedding,' the musicians call to the other boys in the street, because the round dance at a wedding was the men's dance, but the boys aren't interested. They try again. 'Look, here's a dead beetle, let's give it a decent Jewish burial.' This to the girls because the mourner's dirge was the women's part, but the girls also refuse to be led by the band, who by now are thoroughly cross with the others.

Jesus is saying, 'There is no pleasing children in this grumpy mood, try as you like. Neither can I get anywhere with this society. In their eyes I can't do anything right. If God's message is necessarily severe they say, "Lighten up! Where's your sense of humour?" And when I delight in God's generosity and celebrate his boundless love and forgiveness to all people, they complain, "You're flippant and your message shallow." I can't win here.'

Two millennia on and in a world unimaginably different from the Israel of Jesus' time, it seems that similar attitudes exist. Christians here and now can appreciate something of what Jesus was up against there and then. His complaint against 'the people of this generation' resonates with our own experience. We, too, feel that we are on a hiding to nothing at the hands of often unreasonable and nit-picking critics. We are accused of being all sorts of things, and of being none of them. Thus, Christians are said to be too remote from the big issues of the day, but also too involved in them. We are, it seems, too other-worldly and naïve, but also too worldly-wise. We are caricatured as harsh and judgemental in questions of morality, particularly in relation to minority groups (Puritan is the swear word commonly used), while at the same time derided as 'spineless and indecisive' in giving moral leadership in the country. We are ridiculed for the number of older people in our congregations (an odd criticism this, given that 60-year-olds now outnumber 16-year-olds nationally) yet resented for the striking success and popularity of church schools. It appears we just cannot please our critics. 'Damned if we do and damned if we don't' is fair comment.

Critics complain that Christian worship is 'traditional, unintelligible, boring', but the same people glow incandescent with indignation when they discover contemporary worship, which is dynamic, immediate, informal, experimental. 'Where', they then ask, 'is the beautiful roll and rise of Shakespeare's language, where is the reverence and the sense of the numinous, etc., etc.?' So worship is reckoned too formal *and* too free-falling; too gorgeous *and* too plain and drab; there is too much old language *and* too much glossalalia; overmuch openness to the Spirit but also not enough of it. And our preachers must be an amazing lot, 'bookish and highbrow', but also capable of 'dumbing down' (a favourite sneer) the Christian message by popular presentations. We are lampooned as hopelessly shackled to our ancient buildings, but then taken to court for 'abandoning the nation's priceless heritage' when a congregation wants to modify its old stones and mortar to accommodate growth and innovation for mission. Actually, reports of expanding congregations and exciting initiatives tend to terrify the secular-atheistic orthodoxy implicit in much of the media.

All in all there seems to be something odd going on out there. Society is skewed against giving Jesus the benefit of the doubt. There exists a rather sour and grudging pettiness towards him, as though the kids in the playground relish any opportunity to give him a rough handling. Christians can find this a difficult atmosphere in which to live their faith (for we all like to be liked) and need to think long and deep about their stance within it. In the final sentence of his parable, Jesus points the way forward by linking our destiny with his in a startling image. Without warning, he comes out from his disguise as the familiar freelance rabbi figure, and presents himself to us as 'Wisdom': 'But wisdom is proved right by all her children' (Luke 7.35).

The idea of Jesus as the fascinating woman of the book of Proverbs named 'Wisdom' (*hokmah* in Hebrew, *sophia* in Greek), surrounded by her impressive children, is startling but Jesus' Old Testament-minded audiences will have picked up on the term immediately. At the mention of 'Wisdom' the informed Jewish listener detects a click from somewhere around the centre of the Old Testament. A door slides open and the woman who is one of the great personifications of wisdom steps into the room. Even a casual glance over a few of her trademark statements shows what a remarkable lady she is.

Wisdom refuses to be driven off the streets or out of the public square by indifference or hostility; she doesn't cringe among the faithful, hiding in their synagogues or shrines. You won't find her confined to the contemplative life in a monastery in Kathmandu. Against unreasonable and peevish attitudes of society towards Jesus, picking fights like sullen children, the divine wisdom speaks:

> Wisdom calls aloud in the street,
> she raises her voice in the public squares;
> at the head of the noisy streets she cries out.
> (Proverbs 1.20–21)

The street, the market-place, the stock exchange, the football stadium, the entrance to the university and the door to the pub, are where you find Wisdom setting up her soapbox, calling to any who have the sense to listen. Wherever people congregate, she is there:

> Does not wisdom call out?
> Does not understanding raise her voice?
> On the heights along the way,
> where the paths meet, she takes her stand;
> beside the gates leading into the city,
> at the entrances, she cries aloud:
> 'To you, O men, I call out;
> I raise my voice to all mankind.
> You who are simple, gain prudence . . .
> Choose my instruction instead of silver.'
> (Proverbs 8.1–10)

What is Wisdom? In scripture it is sagacity, skill in bringing ideas through to fruitful action; it is not theoretical but practical. Scripture speaks of a wisdom by which the jeweller works precious metal, the mariner's seamanship, the soldier's warcraft. Wisdom is at work when building a fire, a marriage, a congregation, a nation, a cosmos, a way of salvation. Thus, the cross of Christ is called the 'wisdom of God' (see 1 Corinthians

1.22–24) because by it God's plans of redemption are actualized; Jesus is the make-happen mediator who brings divine desires to realization.

Who is Wisdom? Like a certain sort of detective novel we will name names now and through the rest of the book unfold its meanings. The New Testament writers saw all roads leading from the wisdom-writing of the Old Testament (principally Job, Psalms, Proverbs, Ecclesiastes and Song of Songs) to their fulfilment in the person of Jesus Christ. For example, the promises of Proverbs 2.3–4:

> and if you call out for insight
> and cry aloud for understanding,
> and if you look for it as for silver
> and search for it as for hidden treasure . . .

are answered in Colossians 2.2–3: 'Christ, in whom are hidden all the treasures of wisdom and knowledge.'

At the height of New Testament teaching on the person of Jesus (Christology) are these statements in 1 Corinthians 1.

> Christ, the power of God and the wisdom of God. (1.24)
> Christ Jesus, who has become for us wisdom from God. (1.30)

And again in Colossians we are given a stunning paraphrase of 'Christ the wisdom of God'.

> He is the image of the invisible God, the firstborn over all creation. For by him all things were created: things in heaven and on earth, visible and invisible, whether thrones or powers or rulers or authorities; all things were created by him and for him. He is before all things, and in him all things hold together. And he is the head of the body, the church; he is the beginning and the firstborn from among the dead, so that in everything he might have the supremacy. For God was pleased to have all his fullness dwell in him.
> (Colossians 1.15–19)

And if we wish to see more of 'wisdom's' qualifications, look at John 1.1–18, where he appears as the *logos*, the word incarnate in the man Jesus.

A third and rather odd question, before we proceed:

Where did Wisdom learn wisdom? If there is a source of wisdom to which Jesus turned for inspiration, clearly we who claim to be his children must go there. It is an utterly uncanny thought that God's Sophia-Christ, 'in whom are hidden all the treasures of wisdom and knowledge' (Colossians 2.3), was himself formed in skills of wisdom-teaching by meditating on the old scriptures, and observing his local rabbi at work. The serious implication of that suggestion for our own attitude to the scriptures is illuminated by Austin Farrer's remark:

> I read the Old Testament because it is the scriptural inheritance Christ received, it is what he filled his mind with, it is the soil in which his thoughts grew, it is the alphabet in which he spelled, it is the body of doctrine which he took over and transformed.[1]

Our task is to live facing both ways. First towards Sophia-Christ, to wait upon her, study her, her words and ways, both what she says in the Gospels and the way she expresses her thought, the medium and the message. Then to turn and face the world as agents of wisdom, 'to prove her right' by word and action. She entrusts us with the task of vindicating her, proving her right, pointing to the evidence of her presence in the world. Her children are to be out there in the thick of the action, in everything, everywhere, witnessing to Sophia's activity, speaking, arguing, reasoning, defending, explaining, living and enacting her wisdom in public places. It all adds up to a consuming calling which will engage every inch and ounce of our abilities; a breathtaking mission with real and solemn consequences for all concerned, believers and non-believers.

'Proving Sophia right' is a total way of life, a compelling reason to enter each new day in the power of Sophia's Holy Spirit.

Our reflections will take us into aspects of Jesus' teaching that will have the smell of Palestine still on them. We will dare to approach the ravishing teaching of the Lord Jesus Christ as the 'cosmic wisdom' by whom the worlds spin. All true wisdom has its origin and its fulfilment in Sophia-Christ. With each aspect, as we proceed, we will ask the question, 'What will my life look like as I endeavour to prove Sophia right in this?'

> In wisdom's company do all good things come,
> Those who receive her are friends with God.
> (Canticle 26, A song of the spirit of wisdom, *Celebrating Common Prayer*)

Taking it further

When T. S. Eliot contemplated the loss of the God-centred vision in our society he posed three questions:

> Where is the Life we have lost in living?
> Where is the wisdom we have lost in knowledge?
> Where is the knowledge we have lost in information?[2]

They are astonishingly apt for an Internet culture, but do you agree with his analysis? How is it possible to lose wisdom in knowledge?

CHAPTER 2

Wisdom's Charms

You are familiar with those word-association, gut-response games designed to reach behind our considered opinions to our instinctive attractions or aversions. 'What do you feel about it before you think about it?' Some of the brightest in the land make a living trying to read and manipulate the population's gut instincts on behalf of the advertising industry. They talk a lot about trigger words and images which touch nerves and release certain emotions, particularly the 'I must buy that' emotion. Told that you've won a holiday in the Bahamas, staying at the Coral Beach Hotel, those names will trigger ecstasy. But if it's a holiday in Neasden, staying at the Travelodge on the North Circular Road, those names may trigger, well, something a shade less than the ecstatic.

Try this. Take the two words, 'Truth' and 'Wisdom'. Before your orthodox, well-reasoned interpretation of each word kicks in, note your instincts. Does the word make you smile or frown? Does it feel warm or cold? Smooth or harsh? Welcoming or forbidding? Does it evoke curiosity or a yawn? Is it Bahamas or Neasden? Wisdom and truth relate as heat and light from the same sun; they are two aspects of the one Lord Jesus. Wisdom wouldn't be wise if it wasn't also true, and the truth is wise on account of being true. Nevertheless, if my own reactions to each are anything to go by they can conjure quite differing emotions. For myself, 'the truth' immediately evokes an idea of bright, elevated light, priceless but hard, like diamonds. But at the mention of 'wisdom' I feel as if something fascinating and beautiful is up ahead, smiling, intimate, beckoning from out of the centre of things, mysterious but in a profoundly positive and welcoming sense, deeply kind and joyful, like someone who knows an incredibly wonderful answer to our search.

There is a point to these ramblings and it is this: it may be more fruitful when talking with people about Jesus to lead with 'wisdom' rather than with 'truth'. He is indeed the 'Truth', just as he is the Way and the Life, but because of the cultural shift into the chaos known as postmodernity, claims for 'the truth' can stir the waters unnecessarily. They may evoke a puzzled smile, or be taken as a declaration of war, an incitement to near riot. Either way, progress on the subject of Jesus is effectively scuppered. On the other hand, reactions to the idea that Christ is wisdom will be more promising. Without even pausing to define wisdom, the word does 'trigger' interest. Everyone has a wisdom; it figures in some form or other in everyone's outlook on life. Instead of the confrontational, 'That opinion of yours, how does it relate to the truth?', we could question if it's a wise plan for life. We can assume a general acknowledgement that some ways of leading one's life are better, because they are 'wiser' than others; that a 'wisely led life' is happier, that wisdom is a positive force, it is life-building.

There is another encouraging gain to gathering the conversation around 'wisdom'. Seeking wisdom is a journey in which one person's insights are as valid as the next person's. If Christians could refrain from assuming that they know everything in these matters and proceed with a little humility, by asking questions (genuine enquiries) about the other's discoveries, progress can be made. Notice how Jesus used questions. He engaged with a couple of visitors by asking, 'What do you want?' (John 1.38). He doesn't immediately say, 'Come and you will see,' (1.39); that would be to commandeer the moment. Neither does he ask, 'Are you interested in coming to see where I live?', for that would pin them down too specifically – perhaps they are seeking something else. No, his question to them opens the door to whatever those two men want to do next; it is a facilitating invitation, without putting words into their mouths. They are face to face with wisdom incarnate, yet his courtesy and consideration towards them are extraordinary.

We will assume in our contact with people that together with us they are seekers after the wisdom without which real life isn't possible. And surely everyone is aware of the consequences of *un*wisdom, examples of which fill a fair proportion of the media most days. W. B. Yeats wrote:

> We had fed the heart on fantasies,
> the heart's grown brutal from the fare.[1]

Part of Sophia's children's task is to probe the current fantasy-diets, which eventually cause such damage and disillusionment. Again the question is not so much, 'Are they true?', but 'Are they a wise basis for life?' Hence the way Jesus' teaching exposes and demolishes false foundations for life in order to clear the way for the truth. Wisdom constantly raises the disconcerting question of consequences. If you sow this particular seed, what sort of harvest will you reap? What will be the bottom line when all the calculations are done? Before you plunge into that pool, could it just be that it is only a mirage? This splendid house you are constructing, is it standing on rock or sand? If you gain the whole world but at the loss of your soul, would you say that is a good bargain? If you are assembling your life with your back turned to its designer and creator, what are the chances of success? Compassion will fetch a glass of water for a thirsty man, but Wisdom goes further because she knows that when his thirst is quenched, his soul-thirst remains, as nagging as ever. The man who thought that a drink of water was the sum of all his needs now realizes that it isn't.

Keep an eye open for the way events expose unwisdom. One powerful and deeply moving portrayal of the difference between true wisdom and the mere cleverness of the secular interpretation of personal fate is found in Mike Nichols' film *Wit.* Emma Thompson plays a brilliant professor of English Literature whose specialism is the poetry of John Donne. She is dying of ovarian cancer. The film probes the limits of medical science, the intellect and metaphysics. In a final scene, as her inevitable death is closing in, she reflects on the decision which had directed her life and concludes with the heart-breaking words: 'I thought that being extremely smart would take care of it, but I see that I've been found out.' Words which could well stand as an epitaph for our extremely smart but staggeringly unwise society.

Wisdom's children will be faithful enough to draw a friend's attention to the dangers of living in unwisdom, and of the impotence of mere ideas when, as Jesus said, 'The rain comes down, the streams rise, and the winds blow and beat against the house' (Matthew 7.24–27). Coleridge, for all his dazzling ideas, could say this: 'Our quaint metaphysical opinions in an hour of anguish are like playthings by the bedside of a child deadly sick.'[2]

But isn't 'Christ the wisdom of God' one such 'quaint metaphysical opinion'? No, he is act and he is fact. He is all action, completed mission, the source of healing opened. The cross of Christ was no 'quaint metaphysical opinion' but a terrible wood-flesh-iron-blood sin-atoning fact by which God reconciled the world to himself. Everything that oppresses our lives and threatens the loss of our meaning and purpose is in scripture, code-named 'death'. The wisdom which Christ is breaks the power of death by his own death and resurrection. Take Christ away and death would remain the final word on life; your dear ones may put as many floodlights as they like around the edge of your grave but you remain as dead as ever.

Sophia's children will go into each day assuming her presence and activity in all things, in every aspect of life. A letter to *The Times* (28 May 2003), in response to an article on the question 'Why are we all here?', illustrates what we may call the reasonableness of wisdom in the way the world is.

> From Dr Frank S. Rickards:
> Sir Fred Hoyle, the astronomer and developer of the steady-state theory of the Universe put it neatly: 'The idea that life was put together by a random shuffling of constituent molecules can be shown as ridiculous and improbable as the proposition that a tornado blowing through a junkyard might assemble a Boeing 747 from the materials therein.' My own conviction is that this extraordinary dance of life we all enjoy calls out for a choreographer.

If our friends share our conviction that life is dance rather than chance, a story with a beginning and an end, we will urge the reasonable corollary that a story requires a storyteller, and a poem is possible only if there is first the poet. If Wisdom indwells life's reasonableness (she is its source), she is also a witnessing presence in life's madness. More than one commentator has observed that almost the only human soundtrack to the opening footage of *In Memoriam: New York City*, the eyewitness film of the assault on the Twin Towers of the World Trade Center, was, 'Oh, my God! Oh, my God!', over and over again. Not necessarily as an expression of devotion, or an evocation of personal faith, but a soul-deep gasp of the only words vast enough to match the horror of the moment.

The Psalmist said:

> If I go up to the heavens, you are there;
> if I make my bed in the depths [sheol],
> you are there.
>
> (Psalm 139.8)

From the way Sophia speaks of herself, particularly in Proverbs 8, we may be sure that she stands in the mainstream of the action, placing herself in our path as we proceed, all unawares, towards whatever are our own defining moments, our own 'cancer-ward' times, our Twin-Tower experiences. She appears in our thoughts whispering, 'And will this find you out? Extremely smart though you undoubtedly are, are you sure that will take care of it? Isn't it time to seek some real wisdom before it's too late?' When, where, how does she raise her disturbing questions? It seems Sophia's repertoire of communication is unlimited. In the greatest of all the 'wisdom' books, Job despairs of ever hearing from God. The young man, Elihu, responds with this observation:

> God does speak – now one way,
> now another – though man may not perceive it.
> In a dream, in a vision of the night,
> when deep sleep falls on men,
> as they slumber in their beds,
> he may speak in their ears

> and terrify them with warnings . . .
> Or a man may be chastened on a bed of pain . . .
> (Job 33.14–19)

Each one will have their own brush with Sophia-Christ: in the deep imagination, in the conscience, in dreams, or at 3 a.m. when sleep is impossible and all the ghosts and terrors come out to play. But also, so people testify, in crowds, through throw-away remarks overheard, at times of the greatest joy and delight in nature. We can say with certainty that Sophia is not a problem to be solved, but a Person to be adored and desired, totally, like a lover. (We might add here that people are moved to take Sophia seriously when they see her children doing so.)

> Blessed is the man who finds wisdom,
> the man who gains understanding,
> for she is more profitable than silver
> and yields better returns than gold.
> She is more precious than rubies;
> nothing you desire can compare with her.
> Long life is in her right hand;
> in her left hand are riches and honour.
> Her ways are pleasant ways,
> And all her paths are peace.
> She is a tree of life to those who embrace her;
> those who lay hold of her will be blessed.
> (Proverbs 3.13–18)

Enchanting words, which conjure up a sense of meeting in a beautiful, eastern walled garden on a balmy evening. Wisdom has style! She confers style on her children.

This could be the place to start in our desire to 'prove' Sophia before a sceptical world. According to Proverbs' description of her great generosity to all who seek her, we ought to appear to others to be spiritually enriched, confident in who we are and where we are going, people of depth and spiritual substance. We will tell the truth about Sophia-Christ, and confess that we find her enchanting and endlessly fascinating as she takes us from one fresh perspective to another. She is more than we can tell. We breathe a purer air with her, which makes life away from her appear dull and monotonous. At a time when the whole point of existence seems to be more and more a variation on the same old theme of personal pleasure, our part is to demonstrate the joy of 'the man who finds wisdom'. We vindicate Sophia when we outjoy the world. And while society is busy negotiating more and more unrestricted access to more and more hedonism, we can tell of another hedonism, in Christ.

> They feast in the abundance of your house;
> you give them drink from your river of delights.
> For with you is the fountain of life;
> in your light we see light.
>
> (Psalm 36.8–9)

At this point, the wisdom book about the mystery and the power of the love between a man and a woman, Song of Songs, comes into play. It has always provided believers with rich images to describe also communion with Christ.

> Awake, north wind,
> And come, south wind!
> Blow on my garden,
> that its fragrance may spread abroad.
> Let my lover come into his garden
> And taste its choice fruits.
>
> (Song of Songs 4.16)

So now, 'proving Sophia right' becomes 'fragrance spread abroad', the aroma of lives lived under her sway, detected up and down the street, where we work and play (and even in the home!) as the Holy Spirit breathes upon the garden.

Taking it further

How would you explain to a friend the connection between these two statements?

1 The secret of life is to have a good time.
2 The secret of life is to live wisely.

CHAPTER 3

In Wisdom's House

Wisdom has built her house;
she has hewn it out of seven pillars.
She has prepared her meat and mixes her wine;
she has also set her table . . .
'Come, eat my food
and drink the wine I have mixed.
Leave your simple ways and you will live;
walk in the way of understanding.'

(Proverbs 9.1–6)

Sophia has her rival in the city: the goddess of love. You can observe one of her followers (in Proverbs 7) offering her devotions to Aphrodite or Astarte in the cult communion meal, proceeding to its required consummation in sexual intercourse (7.14). Dressed to kill, she is on the prowl for the 'youth who lacked judgment' (7.7). He, poor lad, hasn't a chance, he is 'like a deer stepping into a noose' (7.22). Physically and sacramentally, with him she mimics in her world the ways of her deity in the invisible realm. If Sophia is to make progress among the people of the city she must counter the goddess of love's allurement, enchantment and seduction. Against the attractions of the 'woman of death' – 'her house is a highway to the grave, leading down to chambers of death' (7.27) – Sophia, the 'woman of life', conducts her mission from her great house, which is part family home, theological seminary and outreach centre. She is the forerunner of our 'new' patterns of learning together, eating together, walking together, in the knowledge of the Lord. The door of her house stands wide open, the hospitality marvellous towards any who are serious enough to heed her invitation to come in and learn. It isn't her style to simply post up an 'Open' sign, then sit back and wait for customers to roll in. Neither is it Astarte's method. Her evangelists are busy out and about in the city, alluring, enchanting, seducing, participating in the life of the goddess. So Sophia also goes on the offensive:

> She has sent out her maids, and she calls
> from the highest point of the city.
> (Proverbs 9.3)

Her strategy anticipates Jesus' way of mission throughout the length and breadth of Israel, directing his followers, Sophia's children, to 'prove her right' by going to wherever there are people, 'out to the roads and country lanes and make them come in, so that my house will be full' (Luke 14.23). In this way we are protected from the fashionable error of regarding wisdom as a type of passive, disengaged, oriental mysticism which lulls the unwary into an uninvolved detachment, a false split between wisdom and mission, much favoured in the name of inner serenity in a frantically restless world. Thus Wisdom is falsely perceived as packing her bags and moving out to a pleasant retreat house in the hills. But we have seen already that in fact Sophia hunts out the frantically restless world and there she engages with the crowds.

It is interesting to note in this respect the attitude of that Christian culture whose spirituality is greatly admired among us today as embodying a deep, vibrant wisdom: the Celtic Church. But as Bishop John Finney points out:

> The Celts saw movement as of the essence of the gospel . . . There was a basic understanding that evangelism is linked with a thrust from an area of safety into a potentially dangerous world. Today's Church often wants mission without movement, and it becomes no more than a polite request to the world to come and hear the gospel. When the world just as politely declines the Church is non-plussed and wrings its hands over human obduracy.[1]

As we shall see in later chapters, not only does Wisdom go seeking people, but as wisdom-incarnate Jesus fashioned his matchless forms of teaching to the mind of people.

Sophia goes teaching. The content and conditions of her appeal are set out in a compelling passage:

> I, wisdom, dwell together with prudence;
> I possess knowledge and discretion.
> To fear the LORD is to hate evil;
> I hate pride and arrogance,
> evil behaviour and perverse speech.
> Counsel and sound judgment are mine;
> I have understanding and power.
> By me kings reign
> and rulers make laws that are just;
> by me princes govern,
> and all nobles who rule on earth.
> I love those who love me,
> and those who seek me find me.
> With me are riches and honour,
> enduring wealth and prosperity.
> My fruit is better than fine gold;
> what I yield surpasses choice silver.
> I walk in the way of righteousness,
> along the paths of justice,
> bestowing wealth on those who love me
> and making their treasuries full.
>
> (Proverbs 8.12–21)

The question is, can Sophia overcome (counter-seduce) the fatal attraction of the goddess of love (which we take to symbolize any source of seduction with power to lead minds away from the Lord)? Not until her message is projected forward into Sophia-Christ's ministry: 'Quick! Bring the best robe and put it on him. Put a ring on his finger and sandals on his feet . . . Let's have a feast and celebrate' (Luke 15.22–23). In all directions in the New Testament we meet with Wisdom at work, astonishing in the ways she will enrich people:

> So then, no more boasting about men! All things are yours, whether Paul or Apollos or Cephas or the world or life or death or the present or the future – all are yours and you are of Christ, and Christ is of God.
>
> (1 Corinthians 3.21–23)

> Praise be to the God and Father of our Lord Jesus Christ, who has blessed us in the heavenly realms with every spiritual blessing in Christ.
>
> (Ephesians 1.3)

> . . . who have tasted the goodness of the word of God and the powers of the coming age . . .
>
> (Hebrews 6.5)

Blessings that are summed up (if that were possible) in Christ's first miracle in Cana (John 2.1–11), when he rescued a wedding reception on the brink of disaster by turning ordinary water into extraordinarily fine wine.

We are suggesting that Sophia's gifts will displace Astarte's flashy charms, but only if her children demonstrate and 'prove' them to be utterly desirable. Society has a right to see what Sophia is about before moving into her house. Clearly people who do live in that great house will take on its attitudes and manners, its qualities and outlook; they will absorb the conversation and delight in the music. We can expect to see in those people a certain poise and confidence, the security of home and openness towards whatever Sophia imparts. But are we in fact credible advertisements for life at Sophia's school? Do the people who know us detect that we are under her influence? Does the Church come across to 'outsiders' as possessing wisdom? Whoever coined this little reflection clearly had his doubts about us on that score:

> The graduate with the science degree asks: 'Why does it work?'
> The graduate with the engineering degree asks: 'How does it work?'

The graduate with the accountancy degree asks: 'How much will it cost?'
The graduate with the theology degree asks: 'Would you like chips with that?'

Returning to Sophia's struggle for hearts and minds, it is apparent from the way she speaks that she is out to be even more enchanting than her rivals. Whereas Astarte infects her partners, Sophia comes, 'bestowing wealth on those who love me and making their treasuries full' (Proverbs 8.21). It amounts to a conflict between two kinds of hedonism, Astarte's or Sophia's; Christ's hedonism against the hedonism of the new paganism.

Our criticism of the current spirit of hedonism is that it is crass, banal and too shallow to be satisfying or even thrilling beyond the brief moment. The trouble with our culture is that for all its stupendous self-indulgence, noise and glitz, it simply cannot cope with high-class glory. A vital faith in God is essential for that. (Although in all honesty we must also acknowledge that 'glory' is hardly the first concern in our churches. 'We don't do glory' is not an unfair comment on whole tracts of church life.) But glance again at our two excerpts from Proverbs in this chapter for a reminder that 'glory' sums up the character of Sophia and her house. Glory of that sort, which later will appear among men and women as 'the light of the knowledge of the glory of God in the face of Christ' (2 Corinthians 4.6), cannot be contained within the spiritually threadbare structure of the prevailing secular scepticism. That is the dilemma: we cannot retain the glory without which we cannot live. Christians will therefore take their stand with Wisdom as she offers 'glory'. But how in practice can we get into this subject with our friends?

Perhaps you are familiar with Don Marquis' little poem, 'The Lesson of the Moth'. It is related by Archy, a rather world-weary and disillusioned cockroach who lived inside Don Marquis' typewriter during his days with the *New York Herald Tribune.* Archy would come out at the end of the day when the office was deserted and type out his latest reflections on the way of the world, the meaning of life, Mehitabel the cat and, on this occasion, his conversation with a moth on how much glory a body can experience in one life. It is a very modern allegory:

> i was talking to a moth
> the other evening
> he was trying to break into
> an electric light bulb
> and fry himself on the wires . . .
> we get bored with the routine (said the moth)
> and crave beauty
> and excitement
> fire is beautiful
> and we know that if we get
> too close it will kill us
> but does that matter
> it is better to be happy
> for a moment
> and be burned up with beauty
> than to live a long time
> and be bored all the while . . .
> and before i could argue him
> out of his philosophy
> he went and immolated himself
> on a patent cigar lighter
> i do not agree with him
> myself i would rather have
> half the happiness and twice
> the longevity
>
> but at the same time i wish
> there was something i wanted
> as badly as he wanted to fry himself
> archy[2]

Frankly I would love to say that I am with the moth on this one in his crazy, magnificent dash for glory, except, why does it have to be so brief and so utterly destructive? So I'm inclined to play safe and side with the sensible Archy, although I dread the prospect of dying slowly by inches through the appalling boredom of our present way of life (notice the give-away cry, 'i wish there was something i wanted as badly as he wanted to fry himself').

Christ answers our dilemma by bringing us into the flame of his beauty, which burns not into destruction in a split-second blaze of glory, but into the life of God, eternal life, and for all eternity. Austin Farrer writes on that exchange, God's eternal life for our transience, that it is

> an endless beginning, ceaseless wonder, perpetual resurrection in the unexhausted power of him who everlastingly makes all things new. Be sure of this, there is no coming to the end of God; the more we know of him and his ways, the more avenues will open for further exploration, or revelation, rather.[3]

Taking it further

We have used several perhaps surprising terms to speak of the way Sophia-Christ comes to or comes upon people: as an enchantment, a sort of 'falling in love', an allurement, even as a seduction. Ask among your Christian friends if their experience is of that sort. What does it mean for the way we pray for others?

CHAPTER 4

Wisdom on Time

Everyone has a wisdom of sorts, made up of part experience, part knowledge, part folklore and possibly part superstition. My old grandmother refused to leave her bed for the safety of the air-raid shelter, even when the London Blitz was raging at its worst, for her 'wisdom' told her, 'A bomb with your name on it will get you wherever you are.' She came through unscathed.

Without wisdom in our public life as well as in our personal affairs we are in desperate trouble. It is the truly paramount power in society, showing itself superior to cleverness, wealth and force:

> Do not envy wicked men,
> do not desire their company;
> for their hearts plot violence,
> and their lips talk about making trouble.
>
> By wisdom a house is built,
> and through understanding it is established;
> through knowledge its rooms are filled
> with rare and beautiful treasures.
>
> A wise man has great power,
> and a man of knowledge increases strength;
> for waging war you need guidance,
> and for victory many advisers.
>
> (Proverbs 24.1–6)

What does wisdom do for us in our daily lives? Not just for those iconic-wisdom personalities such as Moses and Isaiah, Paul, Merlin and Gandalf, but for less spectacular mortals such as ourselves struggling to walk with God in our daily experience. Consider this instance of *un*wisdom, in the strange case of the reluctant embryo:

> . . . he is a child without wisdom;
> when the time arrives,
> he does not come to the opening of the womb.
> (Hosea 13.13)

From that delivery-room trauma we learn a vital characteristic of wisdom: it appears within the right timing of things, choosing the right path at the right moment. Wisdom knows the maturity of a thought and its way out of the 'womb' of the mind into the practical world. The wisdom teachers were intensely interested in wisdom's secret of good timing and right direction:

> There is a time for everything,
> and a season for every activity under heaven:
> a time to be born and a time to die,
> a time to plant and a time to uproot,
> a time to kill and a time to heal,
> a time to tear down and a time to build,
> a time to weep and a time to laugh,
> a time to mourn and a time to dance,
> a time to scatter stones and a time to gather them,
> a time to embrace and a time to refrain,
> a time to search and a time to give up,
> a time to keep and a time to throw away,
> a time to tear and a time to mend,
> a time to be silent and a time to speak,
> a time to love and a time to hate,
> a time for war and a time for peace.
> (Ecclesiastes 3.1–8)

Thus, the wisdom-vision of a life isn't static, a fixed photograph, but a pulsating, rhythmic, purposeful movement in our affairs towards the moment of fruitful action.

The New Testament raises the theme to its highest level in

the activity of Sophia-Christ. The word '*kairos*' is used, meaning time as timing and timeliness in events, the fruitful coming together of people, resources, a sense of human need and openness to the Lord's blessing, which surges to a peak. Milk in a saucepan comes to the boil at its *kairos* moment. Sophia's children will 'prove her right' by going into each day assuming *kairos*-rhythms, and living attuned to the Holy Spirit, available to him for participation in his work of bringing things and people together for blessing.

As we read the Gospels, Jesus' mastery of *kairos*-rhythms is evident on every page. Notice how time after time people are drawn to him with their sense of need and openness to his word and touch. The turning of the water into wine at Cana is a classic *kairos* moment (John 2.1–11); telling the disciples where to lower the nets for a great catch is another (Luke 5.1–9); the boy with his 'five small barley loaves and two small fish' is another (John 6.9). At each of these intersecting moments, in which need, resources, and the Lord came together, the time by the clock (*chronos*-time) was irrelevant. What mattered was *kairos*-time, the moment of blessing, as the *kairos*-rhythm surged and peaked, *then* God acted for the people.

> [Jesus] said to the crowd: 'When you see a cloud rising in the west, immediately you say, "It's going to rain," and it does. And when the south wind blows, you say, "It's going to be hot," and it is. Hypocrites! You know how to interpret the appearance of the earth and the sky. How is it that you don't know how to interpret this present time [*kairos*]?
>
> (Luke 12.54–57)

Why does he call them 'hypocrites'? This strikes us as a very harsh comment. Those people went through their days reading and interpreting the signs on the face of nature. They lived by their ability to tell the timing and the timeliness of the days: whether to plough, to sow, or fish, or stay in bed. Well done! Congratulations on living intelligently. But Jesus asks why it is that the same people, who are so *kairos*-literate when it comes to earning a living and making the best of things, are so dull and imperceptive in reading the signs of God's activity in Christ, who is in their presence, at that moment? The application of Jesus' words to our own lives is too obvious to require further comment. Pray for the wisdom, the spiritual intuition, to 'interpret the present time'.

And what was the point in our Lord's display of psychic foresight when he sent his disciples to ask a man for the loan of a donkey, and to another for the use of a room (Matthew 21.1–3; 26.17–19)? It was for their *kairos* education. In fact we can read the entire account of the disciples' half-blind groping towards their mission as a three-year crash course in timing, living within their Lord's masterful *kairos*-strategies. Thus, even after his resurrection, Jesus is back on the job of demonstrating the secret of effective ministry to his nervous followers: 'Throw your net on the right side of the boat and you will find some' (John 21.5–6). Why? Because it will be the pattern of his interaction with them in the future.

With the outpouring of the Holy Spirit upon the disciples at Pentecost, those *kairos* demonstrations leapt to life in their minds. And how shall *we* undertake our mission? Be alert to *kairos*-guidance and participate in what the Lord is setting up. This is how to maintain our sanity within the mayhem of our circumstances. If Christians appear to the world to be pathetically inadequate in numbers, abilities and resources for the incredible task of winning the nations to Christ, we answer, 'We are *kairos* people.' As in the days of the Gospels, so now also, the Lord is here working with both his right and left hands to bring his available, responsive people to intersect with other people in encounters that are surging to peaks of spiritual readiness.

After the Gospel accounts, the Acts of the Apostles goes on to describe the outworking of the *kairos*-principle. How else could a handful of Christians cheerfully go off into a dangerous and hostile world to demand repentance and faith in Christ? On that same principle, the evangelist Philip left a dramatically fruitful healing mission in Samaria – 'with shrieks, evil spirits came out of many, and many paralytics and cripples were healed. So there was great joy in that city' (Acts 8.4–8) – to go to 'the desert road that goes down from Jerusalem to

Gaza' where he encounters an Ethiopian official. How far back in that man's affairs shall we go to trace the origins of *kairos* rhythms? He is a seeking man, and here are resources: a copy of Isaiah's prophecy which someone had sold or given him, and a chariot, which a competent mechanic in Jerusalem had serviced (and fed his horses). The journey was free of hindrance or attack. Thus the Ethiopian makes his way to the right place at the right time where Philip is waiting to help. The Lord draws the encounter together. The man's fascination with the Christ of Isaiah 53, and his sense of spiritual openness which has been simmering, now come to the boil together for his conversion (Acts 8.26–40).

You may say that you never, or seldom, find yourself caught up in such dramatic *kairos*-encounters, but how can you know that? True, we cannot all be in at the crucial moment of conversion, but that moment appeared only because of the preceding moments and the involvement and contribution of who knows how many others along the way – people of faith who by their love and prayer played their part in the surging rhythms of the Holy Spirit. In fact the reality of Sophia-Christ moving in our affairs according to his *kairos*, and drawing us in with him, fills the most unpromising days with quite marvellous possibilities. Christians who live by that vision are well described as a 'community of possibility'.

For our part, all that is required is inner preparation. Hans Urs von Balthasar writes, 'When our strings are well tuned, God can spontaneously play on our soul. And we should aim at nothing more than this: to stretch out toward and be attuned to God.'[1] Another term for sensitivity to and participation in the Holy Spirit is syntonization, as when two instruments, say a cello and a violin, mutually in tune, can set one another vibrating. Thus the more powerful instrument's note is reproduced at a distance in the smaller instrument. So God's tune can be reproduced in us. Now that is a wisdom to live by.

Taking it further

Take time to reflect on the patterns of your daily life. Visualize yourself within each place in turn, in each situation of work and people. As in your mind's eye you visit each phase of your usual day, lift it up to the Lord, praying for his wisdom to be attuned to his *kairos*-rhythms, and for your eyes, ears and imagination to be open and discerning as you move through the day.

CHAPTER 5

Sophia and the Snake Charmer's Fee

Placing the wisdom writings and the Gospels open side by side, it is clear that Jesus was the archetypal wisdom teacher: 'and now one greater than Solomon is here' (Matthew 12.42), and 'You have heard that it was said . . . But I tell you' (see Matthew 5.21–48). Watching him going about his ministry, we see a man who has served his apprenticeship in the art of wisdom-teaching which evolved in old Israel. It was 'the soil in which his thoughts grew' (see Austin Farrer's words in Chapter 1, page 6). Something unfathomably mysterious was happening with Jesus: the knowledge he had of God as God he learned to express in the idiom of village and farm.

His trademark method of story and symbol, aphorism and metaphor, simile and riddle, were also the teaching devices of Israel's wise men: 'Jesus spoke all these things to the crowd in parables; he did not say anything to them without a parable' (Matthew 13.34).

In the old scriptures Jesus found wisdom wisely coined, its form shaped by its content. The way thoughts were expressed was integral to the thought; great care went into the crafting of the sayings. The renowned authority on the wisdom literature, Gerhard von Rad, comments that the wisdom sayings

> are all composed in a poetic form, they are poetry. And in no circumstances can that be considered to be an insignificant, external feature . . . as if it were something added later; rather perception takes place precisely in and with the poetic conception. It is an expression of an intensive encounter with realities or events . . . it is itself a part of this event.[1]

Therefore the poetic character of 'wisdom' is not added later for effect, like the way we may sprinkle hundreds-and-thousands on top of a plain cake to make it more interesting. An architect friend once explained to me that the practice of adding frills and eye-pleasing extra details to an otherwise boring building is known in the trade as 'tarting up the elevations'. Not so in true 'wisdom', where the poetry is inextricably in its textures.

Our own use of language is different because it is conditioned by our predominantly technical culture. We use language as a container, packaging that is to be stripped off and discarded once the statement has done its job by delivering its cargo of information. Once the bullet is fired, the empty cartridge can be discarded. If at the same time the language used is pleasingly expressed, so much the better; that would be an aesthetic bonus but not of primary importance because inferior language would have served just as well. But, says von Rad, 'Israel could not express her experience of reality in this way', and we mustn't forget that wisdom's concern is always with the experience of reality. In a word, words matter.

If we are to 'prove Sophia right' in her teaching, we do well to put ourselves to school with the old wisdom, to look for the principles of its thought, speech and action which Jesus adopted for his own purposes.

We have two references to his wisdom as a child, the first being: 'And the child grew and became strong; he was filled with wisdom, and the grace of God was upon him' (Luke 2.40). This is followed in the same chapter by the famous occasion when his distraught parents eventually found their missing boy, now 12, 'sitting among the teachers, listening to them and asking them questions. Everyone who heard him was amazed at his understanding and his answers' (Luke 2.46–47). Now imagine him, still in his young teens, sitting on the floor of his local synagogue listening to the rabbi expounding, say, from Ecclesiastes. What did he make of this maxim?

> If a snake bites before it is charmed, the snake charmer loses his fee.
>
> (Ecclesiastes 10.11, REB)

Typical of wisdom-speech, the saying conceals as much as it reveals, or rather it conceals on its way to revealing. So why use this form at all? It seems perverse of a teacher deliberately to throw a smokescreen over his words; surely he will strive for clarity and call a spade a spade. If around the next bend the road terminates in a sudden sheer precipice we want big, blunt, shocking and unambiguous warnings. Never mind poetry and subtlety, for heaven's sake tell it as it is! But that scenario doesn't easily translate into the sphere of the spiritual, however much we feel that it should. Students, congregations, neighbours can and usually do walk away from big, blunt, shocking, unambiguous messages. The secret is so to tell the story that the listener is compelled to listen by its intrigue. Don't pepper your story with such phrases as, 'This is the most marvellous/funny/terrible thing you have ever heard!' Rather tell it in such a way that listeners realize for themselves that it is 'the most marvellous/funny/terrible thing they have ever heard'.

A friend recently came upon these words during a Bible study, where the risen Lord Jesus speaks about rewards for faithful Christians at Pergamum: 'I will also give him a white stone with a new name written on it, known only to him who receives it' (Revelation 2.17). My friend was fascinated and teased by its enigmatic strangeness, its apparent unintelligibility. What is the hieroglyphic 'white stone'? For weeks following, each time we met he would start on about the white stone and the mysterious name it bears. Fascinating that that one image could have the power to penetrate so comprehensively the imagination of a very busy IT manager.

Wisdom requires poetic expression (concealing and revealing) to convey its manifold meanings (the white stone is highly poetic). No other form serves, which is why poetry is, among other things, the language of love. So, back to where we left the young Jesus sitting on the floor with his conundrum about unpredictable snakes.

First, what do *you* think it means? The fact that you are intrigued, puzzled, possibly even slightly irritated that you have to spend (waste?) time on this little game, is itself evidence that it is working. The maxim could mean, simply, that in life we are paid by results, which is to see it from where the snake charmer stands. Or it might just be a warning: 'Even apparently safe situations have potential to harm', which is to see it from the snake's point of view. Or more piously: 'Best not do deals with the devil', that primordial serpent. Or it might intend cynical advice: 'Always look for the hidden costs lurking within any deal.' Or the rabbis' long-winded interpretation: 'If the snake bites a man because the charmer failed to charm it, there is no advantage in knowing how to exercise a charm and not making use of it', i.e. if you have gifts and abilities, 'use them or lose them'. Or it might simply be taken to mean, 'Success depends upon foresight.'

Notice what has happened over the last minute or two. The enigmatic nature of the saying has enmeshed us in its meanings. Our various interpretations may all be 'correct', but they are certainly dull and instantly forgettable. But in its snake charmer form the maxim has already snagged in our minds (like my friend and his white stone) and there it stays, compelling our engagement with it. It works like all effective drama, telling only so much and then leaving the audience to fill in the gaps. Although a statement of fact, it enfolds the reader like a question, or a number of questions, mainly about the psychology of the snake charmer, and possibly of the snake. Here it connects with Jesus' teaching methods. It is surprising to discover how few dogmatic statements he made – rather he preferred to set people questions. A great deal of his teaching he delivered in the form of questions. Even the so-called 'pronouncement stories' notoriously leave questions still to be answered, e.g. paying to Caesar what is Caesar's and to God what is God's. In particular, Mark 12.35–37 ('How is it that the teachers of the law say that the Christ is the son of David? . . . David himself calls him "Lord"; How then can he be his son?') depicts Jesus engaging in just this sort of ambiguity. No wonder 'the large crowd listened to him with delight' (12.37). G. B. Caird comments:

> It has been said of the episode at Caesarea Philippi when Jesus asked his disciples, 'Who do people say I am?' (Mark

> 8.27–30), that the question is more significant than the answer. Jesus not only understands that he poses a problem to his contemporaries, he considers it right that he should.[2]

We conclude that if Sophia's children wish to 'prove her right' to people who are, frankly, suspicious of big 'messages', they must learn how to engage through posing questions. And if that sounds like work for preachers and writers (we long for another G. K. Chesterton or C. S. Lewis) then *live* your questions; so live that your spiritual vision and your behaviour raise questions in people's minds about their own lives. Dramatize your wisdom. And speak it also, of course, but in a manner to match the frame of mind of the people you are with. Consider Paul's directions to the Colossian Christians: 'Be wise in the way you act towards outsiders; make the most of every opportunity. Let your conversation always be full of grace, seasoned with salt, so that you may know how to answer everyone' (Colossians 4.5–6).

Thus we are challenged to think about the people we are likely to meet throughout the day ahead and to ponder prayerfully appropriate ways of speaking with them, should the opportunity arise. What are their concerns, anxieties, hopes? What are their interests? For our conversation to be 'full of grace' suggests a touch of life about our words. Jesus said true speech is in fact the overflow of what is already stored in the heart (Luke 6.45). An inner world teeming with interesting thoughts will spill out into interesting talk, but this is not the same as the lazy, self-indulgent 'I always speak my mind', when perhaps your mind at that moment is not fit to speak. 'Seasoned with salt' suggests wholesome, alive, constructive speech, more like a flavoursome Indian curry than bland, safe speech as interesting as yesterday's leftover porridge. In the words of C. F. D. Moule, 'If a Christian is ever difficult company, it ought to be because he demands too much, not too little, from his fellows' responsiveness and wit.'[3]

The proverbial wisdom of the Old Testament was deeply concerned with speaking the right word. First it is the word that comes from listening and observing:

> He who answers before listening –
> that is his folly and his shame.
> (Proverbs 18.13)

Then it is the timely word, the right word, brought out at the right time:

> A word aptly spoken
> is like apples of gold in settings of silver.
> (Proverbs 25.11)

Next there is the quietly thoughtful, restrained word:

> Do you see a man who speaks in haste?
> There is more hope for a fool than for him.
> (Proverbs 29.20)

Fourth, there is the pleasure of kindly words:

> Kind words are like dripping honey,
> sweetness to the palate and health for the body.
> (Proverbs 16.24, REB)

Also, there is the surprising power of the gentle word:

> Through patience a ruler can be persuaded,
> and a gentle tongue can break a bone.
> (Proverbs 25.15)

Then, all right speech and wise living require as their source the fear of the Lord:

> The fear of the LORD is the beginning of knowledge,
> but fools despise wisdom and discipline
> (Proverbs 1.7)

We may even trust God to work in the space between the words which our minds conceive in secret and which then issue in speech.

> To man belongs the plans of the heart,
> but from the LORD comes the reply of the tongue.
> (Proverbs 16.1)

Finally, we might go on to spice up our talk with, 'Have you heard the one about the bankrupt snake charmer?'

Taking it further

Name two or three advertisements that capture your interest by their approach. How do they work on you? To what extent do they 'conceal in order to reveal'? How do they persuade? Should Christians have anything to do with the advertiser's cunning arts?

CHAPTER 6

To Dazzle Gradually

Is J. K. Rowling an admirer of Jesus' teaching method? The question occurred to me a few minutes into the first of the Harry Potter films, when our attention was drawn to the door of an average house in an ordinary street. An eerie atmosphere pervades the house; a sense of something weird about to happen which will have profound consequences for Potterworld. The urgency of that moment could be signalled by any of several well-tried ploys: a banner strung across the street announcing in Day-Glo letters, 'Here today! A very important event!', or a loudspeaker van driving up and down, or a leaflet drop into every home. But these are tough times for advertisers, striving for the attention of a hard-bitten and rather cynical public whose reaction to banner, van or leaflets is likely to be, 'If your news is as urgent as you say, why is your communication so naff?' The medium rubs off on the message.

Instead, an owl flies into the street and sits on a fence opposite that front door. Then a second owl, then more and more, until owls occupy rooftops, trees, telephone wires. Without a word uttered, one look into the face of an owl says it all: that inscrutable, mysterious, wise face. The audience surrenders to intimations of spooky strangeness and spiritual upheavals.

Even a casual reader of the Gospels can see how skilfully Jesus employed 'owls' in his teaching. By his range of speech in parables and aphorisms – wordplay, symbols, humour, riddles, questions – he was able to capture the listener's attention and propel it towards his revelations. We find no long-winded allegories in his teaching, no fables; no fig trees or sheep speak in his stories. Rather they have about them the noise and smell of everyday life, a skill learned in the school of old Israel's thinkers.

> Not only was the Teacher wise, but also he imparted knowledge to the people. He pondered and searched out and set in order many proverbs. The Teacher searched to find just the right words, and what he wrote was upright and true.
>
> The words of the wise are like goads, their collected sayings are like firmly embedded nails – given by one Shepherd.
>
> (Ecclesiastes 12.9–11)

In a masterly passage, Matthew 13, which includes no less than eight parables, Jesus answered his exasperated disciples, who 'came to him and asked, "Why do you speak to the people in parables?"' (13.10). He gave two reasons which leap out at the present day Christian as incredibly relevant to our own mission.

1 Jesus used parables to engage with the semi-interested.

He said to his disciples, 'The knowledge of the secrets of the kingdom of heaven has been given to you [the disciples] but not to them [the crowds]. Whoever has will be given more, and he will have an abundance. Whoever does not have, even what he has will be taken from him' (Matthew 13.11–12).

It appears that the spiritual dynamics of the kingdom have little use for our notions of fair distribution! A person who is growing in the truth is being strengthened, deepened, expanded by that very process, and is thus able to receive more. But where he does not willingly receive God's word, not only does he lose that word, but he is in a process of decline. Too cramped in his interior space, he is unable to retain what he already possesses.

In fact that last phrase is misleading, for in the spiritual life we do not 'possess' life and blessing as though it were a fixture. The committed person (like the disciples in Matthew 13) is one who has come into the light of obedience to Christ and no longer needs to be lured or outwitted into attending to the word; he or she no longer needs to be offered the bait of beguiling pictures, for 'the knowledge of the secrets of the kingdom of heaven have been given to you'.

Once a person makes his way into the orbit of Christ's teaching with an appetite to know more, the next steps are relatively easy. She can join any of the six or so excellent 'basics' courses such as Alpha or Emmaus. She is now among those Jesus described as 'whoever has will be given more'. But Jesus was tremendously concerned about the hoverers who were curious about him but still far from making a decisive commitment – the vast majority in the crowd.

Superficially intrigued, their position is precarious because their engagement with Christ's word, lacking penetration and rooting, cannot survive for long. Hence Jesus' disturbing analysis of the seed's career in the parable of the sower (Matthew 13.1–9, 18–23). The danger period follows the initial, apparently successful impact of the word-seed which is received with joy and enthusiasm but not taken in deeply. Satanic activity will attack the word as it lies, exposed and vulnerable, on top of the mind. At this critical moment only a movement down into depth can save it. Consider the wisdom of W. B. Yeats' words:

> God guard me from those thoughts men think
> In the mind alone;
> He that sings a lasting song,
> Thinks in the marrow-bone.[1]

Left on the mind's surface, the hearer will lose interest in the word as distractions and then boredom go to work; then, 'Whoever does not have, even what he has will be taken from him.' With whatever knowledge we have of Christ's seed-word the principle is, 'Use it, or lose it.'

And here is the greatest challenge to Sophia's children: how to be a bridge between the superficially interested listeners and their full entrance into the kingdom. With 95 per cent of the population outside the fringes of the teaching church, how are they ever to make the move into the sphere of teaching unless they encounter, and are attracted by, Christians scattered throughout society? Effective Christians, getting on with their daily lives, in so doing can act as stepping stones for interested people to progress towards Christ.

We are not concerning ourselves here with the special role preaching fulfils in engaging with seekers. In a sense, the preacher's task is 'easy' – people are coming to him on his home ground. Certainly, some sermons would be more effective if they included a few more 'owls'. Without them a sermon may not be gripping, surprising, compelling enough to compete with the myriad other messages teeming in the brains of the people we meet. But our text, you may remember, reads, '*But wisdom is proved right by all her children.*' Not just the preachers, but the majority who spill out from Sunday church into their Monday-to-Friday week. They hold the key to effective mission. In other words, *each believer and congregation is called upon to live their own parable of the kingdom, in their own sphere and in their own way.*

Our own parable will be fashioned out of the impact of God's grace upon our lives within our local circumstances. A story of forgiveness and love, risk and discovery, holiness and laughter – a coherent story to attract the interest of seeking people and point them on to Christ. If you like the metaphor, the local congregation is an 'experimental garden', demonstrating what the Holy Spirit is capable of growing in lives.

'Parable-speech' is a surprising and creative way in which to enact the kingdom. 'Tell all the Truth, but tell it slant', says Emily Dickinson in a clever poem which is itself a sort of parable about speaking and living in parables. The full truth may be too much for some people to cope with head-on, too bright and intimidating; therefore the truth is more effective if it 'dazzles gradually', by being couched in metaphor:

> Tell all the Truth, but tell it slant
> Success in circuit lies
> Too bright for our infirm Delight
> The Truth's superb surprise.
>
> As Lightning to the Children eased
> With explanation kind
> The Truth must dazzle gradually
> Or every man be blind.[2]

We are not saying that 'gradual dazzle' is the only way, for God will not be tied by any of our theories on how he works.

'Damascus road' experiences are also happening, but if the results of the surveys are to be trusted the great majority of adults coming to personal faith come 'gradually'. Gerard Manley Hopkins beautifully expressed God's freedom to reach people as he will:

> With an anvil-ding
> And with fire in him forge thy will
> Or rather, rather than, stealing as Spring
> Through him, melt him but master him still:
> Whether at once, as once at a crash Paul,
> Or as Austin*, a lingering-out sweet skill,
> Make mercy in all of us, out of us all
> Mastery, but be adored, but be adored King.[3]
> *Austin is Augustine

2 *Jesus used parables to reach the people who do not yet understand but think they do!*

And to demolish false notions of God in order to build true ones. He described this category of listener as,

> Though seeing, they do not see;
> though hearing, they do not hear or understand.
> (Matthew 13.13)

Unbelief is at least relatively clear; wrong-headed belief is much more difficult to address. How do you help a sick man who is quite sure he is well? In a striking image Isaiah describes the dilemma:

> as when a hungry man dreams he is eating,
> but he awakens and his hunger remains;
> as when a thirsty man dreams he is drinking,
> but he awakens faint, with his thirst unquenched.
> (Isaiah 29.8)

Jesus laid the explosive charge of parable, both verbal and acted, at the door of the deluded man to awaken him out of his fantasies – parables which say 'No' before they say 'Yes'. In a culture of intensely held religious views, Christ's listeners were, quite unconsciously for the most part, filtering his revelation through their own established views of God, which is every preacher's nightmare. There is a theory of communication called the 'silver bullet', which goes like this: prepare your message (the silver bullet) and load it into the 'gun' of your speaking expertise. Aim it at the audience and fire it into their brains where it will be fully absorbed and understood. It is, of course, a total fantasy. People hear only (or mostly) what they want to hear and which agrees with what they already know and believe.

Jesus employed his parable-speech because he understood full well the fallacy of the 'silver bullet'. First he had to deal with the problem of entrenched warped ideas of God. Therefore he sent in his 'owls', his words and acts, to awaken the dreamers and subvert the complacent. In one marvellous incident two parables were used for the task, one enacted and the other spoken, in Luke 7.36–50.

A woman 'who had lived a sinful life in that town' (7.37) well and truly put the cat among the rabbinical pigeons when she gatecrashed a Pharisee's party to get close to Jesus. Here begins her dramatized parable, although in fact it had begun earlier, with her determination to get into that room, and unfolded through her ingenuity and courage. There followed a breath-taking expression of gratitude and devotion to Jesus, breaking all the taboos in the process, covering his feet with her tears and kisses and perfume, then wiping them with her hair. Simon's indignation, based upon his theology, was genuine. What is God like? Simon believed that he is a kosher deity who abhors all contact with moral failures (7.39). The woman's lived parable flushed out into the open Simon's deeply held view and allowed Jesus to explode it with a short, lucid story about debt and forgiveness, law and grace (7.40–43). What is God like? He is the boundlessly generous father who freely forgives our debts to him and delights to receive in return the outpourings of our love.

Once again, the punchline was left for the audience to

supply as Jesus set Simon one of his devastating questions (7.42–43).

Taking it further

An urgent task for Sophia's children: draw up a list of the five top 'distorted ideas about God' currently doing the rounds, and work out how to challenge and demolish them prior to rebuilding in the truth. This is, of course, a top priority job for the whole church.

CHAPTER 7

Along the Plateau

A phone call from an old friend has rather disrupted our original plan for the next few chapters. A lady in her eighties, she is recovering after a nasty accident and several weeks in hospital. With her husband (they are both doctors) she spent most of her life working in hospitals and clinics, as well as planting churches, in China and Thailand. As we talked about the physical and spiritual shock of such an accident, I found myself wondering, 'Is this a *kairos*-phone call, a timely reminder of an aspect of wisdom we're in danger of overlooking?' For not only is Sophia 'proved right by all her children', but it is also how those children move on with her decade after decade. While it is wonderful to see young people coming under Sophia's sway it is, if anything, even more impressive to see people putting their full weight on her promises throughout a long life.

Incidentally, what age is the Sophia of the Proverbs? She has all the verve of a vital, charismatic woman who carries the wisdom of God. The Church as described by the early writer, 'The Shepherd of Hermas', was an old lady with white hair, whose flesh was getting younger and younger. Even in her most youthful appearance her hair was still completely white, to show that she was eternally young, yet older than the world. (L'Oréal would kill for the formula!) Did 'The Shepherd' base his picture on the woman of the Proverbs?

We must set limits to our reflections on wisdom and ageing. No reference here to many of the things that are proper concerns in the process of growing older. No advice here on how to oil your Zimmer frame or how wide wheelchair access should be at church, which exercise bike to get for your forty-eighth birthday, or where to bulk-buy supplies of Co-Enzyme Q10 to boost flagging energy levels, or when to forsake botoxing the wrinkles in favour of the cosmetic surgeons' arts. For answers to such questions and many more, consult *Saga* magazine. But no one will seriously expect that excellent publication to advise its readers on how to emulate the apostle Paul's wisdom for growing older as 'I press on towards the goal to win the prize for which God has called me heavenwards in Christ Jesus' (Philippians 3.14). Or Judah Helevi's thrilling vision of travelling this life:

> I am running towards the fountain of true life;
> Therefore I spurn the life of lies and trifles.
> To look at the face of my King – that is my only wish,
> None but him do I fear and venerate.[1]

This is what is meant by wisdom's 'redeeming' interpretation of the ageing effects on our senses, powers, and all the manifestations of personal life. Without this transmuting vision, which can bring something valuable out of dull, negative circumstances, we are doomed to be no better than merely secular, making the best of whatever hand is dealt to us by 'nature', or chance, or whatever. Then time running out is either a robber or a millstone, and either way a cheat.

Ageing isn't an illness or a failure, although some Monday mornings it can feel like both. Nor is it a cruel riddle such as, 'Why does the Author of the Play set such difficult lines for us to say?' Ageing is as natural as youthfulness but more mysterious and possibly scarier, though in a different way: the scariness of the last chance rather than youthful profligacy with countless chances. For one thing, in later life precious possessions spill out through fraying seams in our baggage – time, friends and energies. As the old woman lamented, 'Since Penelope Noakes of Duppas Hill is gone there is no one who will call me Nellie again.'

The simplest sketch of our development and progress looks something like this: there is the carefree romp in the childhood meadows, leading out and up to the exuberant dash through the foothills of adolescence. The track climbs steeply until it levels out at 'maturity' – welcome to the plateau of manhood or womanhood. The rest of our days are spent on the long walk across the plateau until we reach a time and a place where the ground falls away under our feet. Eventually, quietly in a nursing home, if we are lucky, the this-world episode of our story is done and the transfigurations of eternity begin.

Now rewind the tape to around halfway along the plateau to where walkers enter the phase known in sociologist-speak as 'the ageing process'. Odd jargon, as though before mid-plateau we were merely growing older, but now we are officially ageing. And yet a qualitative difference happens at this time as much in the mind as the body; it is a time of elusive but real alterations and shiftings. Muscles and joints send their urgent shrieks up to the brain, 'Steady on! Is this wise? Act your age!' Another clue may be that members of the opposite sex no longer bestow appreciative glances in your direction. Careful here, because any blow to your vanity at this age could trigger the famous 'mid-life crisis' and bizarre acts of rash folly. How sad is Mary Anne Sieghart's comment that her 'friends who have hit 50 say men look through them as if we're not there'.

Mid-life feels as though a shadowy stranger has slipped into the house through a basement window (and left the window open – we feel the draught) and is slowly ghosting his way up to the top floor. Predictions of middle age lurking up ahead had always seemed too remote and unreal to take seriously, like rumours of an earthquake in Outer Mongolia. Yet here it is, we've been rumbled and life will never be the same. Now we are among those classed as 'getting on a bit' and, with an embarrassed and apologetic little laugh we explain ourselves as 'not quite as young as we used to be'. This is life at mid-plateau, facing autumn.

With 60-year-olds outnumbering 16-year-olds nationally there is an awful lot of ageing going on out there – masses of mellowing, mid-to-later plateau walkers enjoying their new longevity. They are that 'demographic time-bomb' which causes the Chancellor of the Exchequer sleepless nights over pensions, etc. It is a mystery, therefore, why in the churches we seem to give only slight attention to the wealth of experience, faith, gifts and wisdom gathering down the greying end of the plateau. Perhaps in this, as in too much else, we take our lead from the world, which can seem equally indifferent to these opportunities: only 5 per cent of British advertising spending is aimed at people over 50, who are in fact responsible for more than 45 per cent of disposable income (*Financial Times*, October 2002). This could be taken as a backhanded compliment, as advertisers acknowledge older people's resistance to changing their favourite breakfast cereal. 'Concentrate on the kids – they'll believe anything!'

What does Wisdom say of our trek along the plateau? She teaches us to reject current embarrassment over what is the only certain fact in our lives – 'the end' – and to recover the biblical wisdom about 'the remaining time'. When Sir Winston Churchill left instructions for his funeral arrangements he referred to them as 'Operation Hope Not'. The gospel is infinitely more positive. From the perspective of Christ's triumph over the physical reality, and the spiritual regime we call 'death', Wisdom speaks. Here are a couple of her insights:

1 Prepare while you are still fit enough to prepare.

That extraordinary wisdom teacher Koheleth (Ecclesiastes 1.1) 'looks out on life with wide open eyes, hating hypocrisy and show, despising injustice and wrong. He knows the sadness of things, but the mood of dejection never freezes over him. Thus he can speak of the joy and beauty of life and set it against the haunting echo of the world's vanity,' says Rabbi Cohen.[2] Koheleth wrote his unique allegory on the ills of old age, a not-too-difficult-to-decode riddle, as a wake-up call to his readers to 'remember' before they are too feeble to remember anything at all. Sort out your life, now, while you still have the energy to do so. It is time to put first things first and to set your life on the way to wisdom. Work out your spiritual strategy, now, while you still have your wits about you.

> Remember your Creator
> in the days of your youth,
> before the days of trouble come
> and the years approach when you will say,
> 'I find no pleasure in them' –

before the sun and the light
and the moon and the stars grow dark,
and the clouds return after the rain;
when the keepers of the house tremble,
and the strong men stoop,
when the grinders cease because they are few,
and those looking through the windows grow dim;
when the doors to the street are closed
and the sound of grinding fades;
when men rise up at the sound of birds,
but all their songs grow faint;
when men are afraid of heights
and of dangers in the streets . . .
Remember him – before the silver cord is severed,
or the golden bowl is broken;
before the pitcher is shattered at the spring,
or the wheel broken at the well,
and the dust returns to the ground it came from,
and the spirit returns to God who gave it.
(Ecclesiastes 12.1–7)

Incidentally, the friend who set us off on this detour into 'wisdom for life along the plateau' was able to manage her depression by recalling to mind the many verses, psalms and passages of scripture which she had 'by heart' (wonderful phrase!). 'In the days of her youth' she had, literally, 'remembered her creator', and now felt supported by a sense of her creator remembering her in his words. But, warns Koheleth, if we will not stir ourselves to the hard work of 'remembering' (and committing to memory) while we are able, expect gloom to close in on the ageing mind.

'Meaningless! Meaningless!' says the Teacher.
'Everything is meaningless!'
(Ecclesiastes 12.8)

He isn't pouring on the pessimism here, merely doing what a good teacher must do by being realistic. Look around you for confirmation of his analysis. It is sensible to make reasonable preparations for life down the far end of the plateau, but it would be the ultimate instance of 'arranging the deckchairs on the *Titanic*' if we do not also take the teacher's wisdom to heart and give serious thought to our next big move.

2 Save the present for the future.

When wisdom-teaching concerning the creative use of 'the remaining time' is taken forward into Christ the result is life-transforming. Jesus said:

> Do not store up for yourselves treasures on earth, where moth and rust destroy, and where thieves break in and steal. But store up for yourselves treasures in Heaven, where moth and rust do not destroy, and where thieves do not break in and steal. For where your treasure is, there your heart will be also.
>
> (Matthew 6.19–21)

Our Lord is *not* saying that only certain activities are 'treasure for heaven', for that would give special categories of people a flying start over the rest of us. Storing treasure in heaven does not single out our 'spiritual' acts – prayer, missionary work – while the 'ordinary' round of daily duties (which is where most of us spend most of our lives) are 'treasures on earth'. *'Treasure in heaven' is any and every action which is done for the love of God.*

Augustine gives a lively illustration of this truth. He describes himself gathering apples in from his orchard, taking them into his barn and setting them out on the floor. A neighbour comes in and protests that what Augustine is doing is the surest way to lose them to rats and mould. 'What shall I do?' Augustine asks. His friend tells him, 'Get them off the floor up on to high shelves where they're safe.' There are not two sorts of apples, only one – which can either stay on the ground and rot or be lifted up and preserved. Our lives are one 'treasure', not two; we are not made up of 'holy' sections and 'ordinary' ones. Everything constitutes our 'treasure', the output and sum total of our lives. And everything about our lives is capable of being stored 'on earth' or, the same things 'in heaven'. The *deciding factor is love for the Lord.* Anything and everything is transmuted from being merely what it is into 'treasure in heaven' when offered up to the Lord with the intention, 'I do this for you, Lord – accept this with my love.' Thus the entire sweep of our lives may be saved from disappearing into the sand and sent up to heaven where the Lord says, 'Thank you! I've got it safe. I'll keep it here with me until you come.'

What we do is not the point, because what we do is largely determined by circumstances and duty. What we do changes with age. What matters is that 'the time remaining' is raised off the floor and sent up ahead. Not what we do but *for whom* we do it. You can decide to start now, and renew the decision tomorrow, and again the next day and the next, and so 'save' the output of your life in loving the Lord.

Taking it further

The secret of a successful journey across the plateau to its end is simple but elusive. George Herbert grasped it in his wonderful words:

> Wherefore with my utmost art
> I will sing thee,
> And the cream of all my heart
> I will bring thee.[3]

Take time to consider if the God-adoring movement of his life is true of yours also.

CHAPTER 8

Expanding the Soul-Space

Trust a Frenchman to throw a spanner in the works! But when that Frenchman is the wise Bernanos we do well to attend to his thoughts on our theme of 'wisdom for travelling the plateau'. But there's the snag (or the spanner), for he objects to our picture in the previous chapter of adult life as a walk across the plateau between adolescence and age. Bernanos is unhappy with the idea of 'maturity', which he thinks is a myth cooked up by the sociologists.

> The 'mature man' is a legendary animal . . . he does not exist because there is no neutral stage between youth and old age. He who cannot give more than he receives is already starting to decay. Even a careless observer can see that a miser at twenty is already an old man.[1]

There is, he believes, no plateau, 'no neutral stage between youth and age'. You live in one condition or the other. The 60-year-old can live in youthfulness and the younger person can already be decrepit. The deciding factor is *generosity,* giving more than we receive.

As you sit there reading this page, you are either climbing in spiritual youthfulness, or declining into spiritual ageing and decrepitude regardless of the date on your birth certificate. Which one? That depends on whether you are a giver or a taker. The givers are young; the takers are old. Therefore the catalyst of spiritual decay is not necessarily something darkly sinister, but quite simply mean-mindedness. Everyday encounters with our fellow-citizens confirm the wisdom of Bernanos' observations. Truly generous people do have liveliness about them, a sort of lightness of spirit as if they are not afraid to part with something of themselves. We enjoy being near them; they are like a comfortable chair by a warm fire in cold weather.

On the other hand, it is as though something vital had never been switched on inside the head of the mean-spirited individual. He seems closed off (or closed-down), living in his inner room with the blinds permanently drawn, or like a cracked bell, which clatters but gives out no resonant ring. Suspicious, critical, quick to believe the worst of another, niggardly, narrow-hearted and tight-fisted, 'a miser at twenty is already an old man'. There is a humility about the generous person who is open and encouraging towards other people, just as there is a certain arrogance about the mean-minded person who presumably does not rate other people worthy of his interest:

> The arrogant person is like a black object. In order to acquire some energy and thus be able to 'shine', he sucks up all the light into himself; not knowing that precisely because of this he no longer reflects a single ray and so is wholly darkness. The humble person is already bright: whatever he receives he passes on, and he shines precisely because he does not clutch at things. Because he readily transmits the borrowed light that falls on him, he himself becomes light. Love and mission are one.[2]

Balthasar's fine words describe the wisdom by which we grow away from soul-decay and grow into spiritual youthfulness.

On television last night a man was explaining how wonderfully well his retirement was proceeding: 'We have four holidays in the year, and I play golf three times a week.' Well, why not, if he has worked hard all his life for it, but I couldn't help contrasting his attitude with that of a woman in our congregation (yet another in her eighties!). Recently her surgeon gave her two pieces of news: first, without a particularly complex heart operation she will very soon die; and, second, he was not prepared to attempt the operation because of the dangers involved. Her response was to go out and sign up with a church group taking financial gifts to impoverished Christians in Ramallah. She is always one of the 'givers', a living proof of the vitality and youthfulness of those who practise Christ's generosity. It is the special gift of older Christians to demonstrate this wonderful alternative, and to show the durability of wisdom. A friend writing from the United States mentions meeting Paul Brandt again after many years. Paul Brandt was the first surgeon in the world to use reconstructive surgery to correct deformities in the hands and the feet caused by leprosy. My correspondent describes Paul Brandt, now in his eighties (what is it about these amazing octogenarians!), as 'sharp, gracious and above all still active in Christian work'.

Jesus took the issue further when he describes the enlarging effect of generosity on the giver himself:

> Do not judge and you will not be judged. Do not condemn, and you will not be condemned. Forgive, and you will be forgiven. Give, and it will be given to you. A good measure, pressed down, shaken together and running over, will be poured into your lap. For the measure you use, it will be measured to you.
>
> (Luke 6.37–38)

Use as large a scoop ('measure') as possible when giving to others from your resources, and the Lord will return the same to you, measure for measure. In your estimation of others be big-hearted – go the second mile . . . give away your coat . . . turn the other cheek . . . forgive countless times – and the Lord will look upon your weaknesses and foibles with mercy and understanding. Practise generosity in argument; be willing to yield as much as possible if it helps preserve friendship, even when you are sure that your position is superior. Not many issues are worth the break-up of friendship and unity. To forgo the pleasure of wiping the floor with your opponent by your brilliant reasoning is asking an awful lot, but the apostle Paul does ask it. He demands it of us: 'Accept him whose faith is weak, without passing judgment on disputable matters . . . Therefore let us stop passing judgment on one another . . . Let us therefore make every effort to do what leads to peace and to mutual edification' (Romans 14.1, 13, 19).

George Herbert, in his lovely peaceable way, comments on the wisdom which preserves harmony: 'He that cannot forgive others breaks the bridge over which he himself must pass; for every man has a need to be forgiven.'[3]

Generosity of mind and behaviour expand our own soul-space, making more room to receive God's gifts. 'Give and it will be given to you' is the secret of a richly teeming inner life, constantly replenished as our expenditures and the willing export of our resources of energy, affection and time are answered by the Father. Any generosity of yours is more than matched by overflowing blessings spilling out all over the floor of your inner room. It all sounds rather like a joke played on our greedy acquisitive, covetous culture; another instance of 'the foolishness of God is wiser than man's wisdom' (1 Corinthians 1.25). The joke might be lost on the philosophers at the CBI or the TUC, for its perspective reaches far beyond the limitations of this world: 'Remember when you leave this earth, you can take nothing with you that you have received – only what you have given: a full heart enriched by honest service, love, sacrifice and courage' (Francis of Assisi).

The Christian is pictured as a perpetual giver who discovers he is caught up in a delightful game, the idea of which is to outdo God in generosity! Here is the wisdom of continual renewal by the hilarious inversion of consumerism's dearest principle: 'I am what I have' becomes 'I keep what I give'.

With another vivid wisdom-metaphor Jesus heightened still further the life-shaping consequences of generosity or stinginess. He said:

> Your eye is the lamp of your body. When your eyes are good, your whole body is full of light. But when they are bad, your body also is full of darkness. See to it, then, that the light within you is not darkness. Therefore, if your whole body is full of light, and no part of it dark, it will be completely lighted, as when the light of a lamp shines on you.
>
> (Luke 11.34–36)

In the understanding of the ancient world the eye was the window for light to enter and illuminate the 'house' of the person's interior life. A 'good eye' is one free of cataracts and diseases. As a spiritual metaphor it signifies transparency and true simplicity of character, straightforwardness, honesty and sincerity. What particularly interests us is that the word 'good' also has the idea of *generosity*. The generous person can 'see' because his eyes are good, sound and clear. Light enters his life with extraordinary effect, so that 'your whole body is full of light, and no part of it dark'. He is irradiated with light, becoming as it were incandescent, 'completely lighted, as when the light of a lamp shines on you', suggesting that even your external appearance is lit up. You become a source of illumination for others. Such is the effect of a generous heart. Of course, 'generosity' isn't itself the light, for that is the life and blessing of God by his Holy Spirit, but the 'good eye' of the truly generous life allows the presence of God to flood that person's inner world.

Conversely, the 'bad eye' of Jesus' parable blocks out the light like a shuttered window. Physically it refers to cataracts and other disorders. Spiritually the 'bad eye' signifies false complexities, hypocrisies, deviousness and double-dealing with God and neighbour. And 'bad' carries also the idea of grudging, mean, tight-fisted, critical and sour attitudes (the 'evil eye') which plunge the owner's own inner household into twilight. Everyday experience proves the truth of this teaching. No doubt you have at some time or another been on the receiving end of 'bad eye' attitudes when you have found yourself quite unable to 'get through' to someone because of their bias against you. You could almost see the shutters come down, their mind's door closing against you for whatever reason. Job interviews are notorious for this sort of treatment. When we look with a 'good eye', with a bias towards giving the other person the benefit of the doubt, that attitude allows him or her to come through to you. It carries risks, of course – the possibility of being taken for a ride – but it saves us from the far more grave risk of self-inflicted blindness through mean-mindedness. Even worse, says Jesus, 'see to it, then, that the light within you is not darkness', for the niggardly soul loses the ability to know the truth about itself. It is difficult to think of a more dangerous delusion than to mistake one's darkness for 'light', but such is the complacent arrogance of hard-heartedness.

So much for the effects of the generous mind on others, as well as within ourselves. This issue is clearly so crucial for our attempt to pursue wisdom that it is worth taking a moment to enquire 'Why?' What is it about a life fashioned around personal generosity that keeps one climbing in spiritual youthfulness? The answer must be that true generosity of spirit resonates with something at the heart of God. In their breathtaking doctrine of the 'Perichoresis' the Church fathers saw the Father, Son and Holy Spirit giving themselves to each other in boundless self-bestowing. What each has, he has for the sake of the others. Trinitarian life ecstatically flowing between one another overflows into creation. The world, the cosmos, all things, exist because God is in his very essence self-outpouring love, continuing out into the incarnation of Jesus the Son, and then into the creation of the Church. Their superabundant overflowing of life and blessings continues out to ourselves, and through us as outlets and channels of the divine generosity out to our local world. Our part in this incredible drama is to reach out in gratitude and love to God's generosity. To live tuned to the heart of God is our wisdom: givers more than takers.

> The person who reaches out for what lies ahead of him is always becoming younger than himself.
>
> (Bishop Basil)

Taking it further

Note on a sheet of paper the different groups of people with which you connect: family, friends, work, neighbourhood, church. Next, reflect on your relationships with the people in each group under two headings: 'Giving' and 'Taking'. Are you more of a giver than a taker? Bring your conclusions to the Lord in prayer, asking forgiveness for hard-heartedness, and praying for fresh immersions in the overflow of Christ's inexhaustible love.

CHAPTER 9

Sophia and the 'Continual Feast'

'Middle-age?' said a schoolteacher friend in response to my question (he is still on the safe side of mid-plateau). 'Isn't that when Mr Grumpy kicks in?' Hoping for insights just a touch more profound, I reached for W. H. Auden's book of aphorisms.[1] This was more promising. 'There is more felicity on the far side of baldness than young men can possibly imagine', puts the teacher in his place rather nicely. 'The first forty years of life give us the text, the next thirty supply the commentary' will appeal to expository preaching types. A little more worrying is the observation, 'After a certain age, the more one becomes oneself, the more obvious one's family traits become.'

For my money the most pleasing of the aphorisms is, 'Nothing is more beautiful than cheerfulness in an old face', and now you can see where this is taking us. 'Wisdom' for the long trek, going all the way to the far end of the plateau, with generosity and cheerfulness, is a wisdom to live by. Sophia is the best companion for the journey, for she brings her joy with her.

'Cheerfulness in an old face'. Is that more beautiful, say, than the happiness in the face of a child? This isn't a beauty contest between grandparent and grandchild, for there is a cheerfulness appropriate to each end of life. We suspect that a child's carefree joy is just that – free of care, free to flourish within parental love. It is the unquestioning cheerfulness of untried and uncluttered innocence, free of adult complexities and hypocrisies. At the other end, 'cheerfulness in an old face' is attractive and intriguing because of its implicit drama. Here is a person who has come through goodness knows what trials and tribulations gloriously uncynical. We are not concerned here with the cheerfulness due to the accident of happy genes and a sunny disposition, but of character hard won.

Like moths to a flame we are drawn to happy people who seem to possess the magic touch. We like to be near them in the hope of contracting a little of that magic. For a person to go all the way to the wire sustained by a joyful inner life is a sure sign that she has cracked the code for living. The biblical wisdom-teachers believed the effects of a cheerful heart were fundamental to well-being. They reveal a strikingly 'modern' understanding of health and sickness as rooted in psychosomatic relationships, insights that later gave Jesus clues to his people's view of the good life.

'A happy heart makes the face cheerful' (Proverbs 15.13)
The related Jewish writing of 'Ecclesiasticus' (*not* Ecclesiastes) enlarges on our verse.

> It is a man's heart that changes the look on his face,
> either for better or for worse.
> The sign of a happy heart is a happy face.
> (Sirach 13.25–26)

William McKane comments on these verses: 'Inner happiness is reflected in the lines of the face, the glow of health as it is visible in the face and the eyes is an epiphenomenon of a healthy and happy mind.' Always realistic, the Proverbs verses also acknowledge the grinding struggle of a life of poverty, while at the same time refusing to be blackmailed into non-cheerfulness by hardship, for, 'Man does not live by bread alone, and there is another kind of nourishment which will sustain him and enable him to conquer.'[2]

It is not indecent to go cheerfully through a world that contains so much crying injustice. On the contrary, a true cheerfulness bears witness to the light and the possibility of another way of seeing things. The world has quite enough misery of its own without adding false Christian misery to it! John Wesley said, 'Sour godliness is the Devil's religion!' G. K. Chesterton was convinced that 'Joy is the gigantic secret of the Christian.'

'A heart at peace gives life to the body' (Proverbs 14.30)
This order is commonly reversed in the expectation that a well cared for physical and material life will 'soak' through to the inner core and so produce a 'heart at peace', the source of joy. No one would deny that having the wherewithal for the family's requirements diminishes anxiety vastly. So why then is 'angst' still one of the defining words of our relatively affluent society? Comfort and ease, yes; but joy and cheerfulness are not words that leap to mind when looking into our world. If cheerfulness is to become a thing of character, rather than a spin-off of whim and mood and dependent upon circumstances, we must attend to what is happening in 'the heart'. In the biblical understanding the state of the heart dominates every manifestation of life. Its activities are mental and spiritual rather than emotional – which is how we usually regard the heart, as the place of warm, sincere feelings. The heart is intended for *understanding* (see Deuteronomy 29.4, where 'mind' translates the Hebrew 'heart') and fullness of perception. 'To think with the heart' sounds odd to our ears, but it is the scriptural usage. Coleridge spoke about 'feeling his thoughts' and advised that we meditate on truths, 'that some time or other they may become your feelings'.[3] Which is why Solomon proved his wisdom by asking God not for ephemeral gifts like riches, fame or longevity but for that which is the source of true living, 'a hearing heart' (see 1 Kings 3.9–12).

Our verse praises the priceless blessing of 'a heart at peace' (Proverbs 14.30): a tranquil and calm heart (mind), a heart that imposes harmony within our inner world, like a masterful conductor who brings to order an ill-disciplined orchestra and even manages to coax some beautiful music from it. First, the heart at peace, and only then come harmony and well-being. Its meaning is further illuminated by the second part of the verse, set in opposition to the first lines.

> A heart at peace gives life to the body,
> but envy rots the bones.

Envy is an expression of a wider dis-ease we experience as restlessness. Compelled to choose one word to describe the spirit of our culture it would have to be 'restlessness'. This is not to criticize the drive of proper ambition, the desire to do things better and to see progress for our efforts. It is more a matter of shifting away from the original centre and the source of our life, by refusing God the adoration of our hearts. No one describes the resulting confusion better than W. B. Yeats when he speaks about his heart as:

> . . . sick with desire
> And fastened to a dying animal
> It knows not what it is.[4]

Ejecting God from his rightful place in our lives we claim 'freedom', only to fall prey to the next plausible idea to come along. The result is a perpetual jostling for control and the rise of impatience, distractedness, envy, discontent – i.e. restlessness – and out goes any hope of a 'heart at peace' with its gifts of 'life to the body'. Henri Nouwen wrote this about the malaise:

> One of the most obvious characteristics of our daily lives is that we are too busy. We experience our days as filled with things to do, people to meet, projects to finish, letters to write, calls to make, and appointments to keep. Our lives often seem like over-packed suitcases bursting at the seams. In fact, we are almost always aware of being behind schedule. There is a nagging sense that there are unfinished tasks, unfulfilled promises, unrealized proposals. There is always something else that we should have remembered, done or said. There are always people we did not speak to, write to, or visit. Thus, although we are very busy, we have a lingering feeling of never really fulfilling our obligations . . . Beneath our worrying lives, however, something else is going on. While our hearts and minds are filled with many things, and we wonder how we can live up to the expectations imposed upon us by ourselves and others, we have a deep sense of unfulfilment. While busy with and worried about many things, we seldom feel truly satisfied, at peace, at home. A gnawing sense of being unfulfilled underlies our filled lives . . . The great paradox of our time is that

> many of us are busy and bored at the same time. While running from one event to the next, we wonder in our innermost selves if anything is really happening. While we can hardly keep up with our many tasks and obligations, we are not so sure if it would make any difference if we did nothing at all. While people keep pushing us in all directions, we doubt if anyone really cares. In short, while our lives are filled, we are unfulfilled.[5]

The spirit of restlessness thrives on drawing our essential selves out onto the surface so that we become, more literally than we thought possible, 'superficial'. True joy is not possible here. The first priority is to do the one thing necessary to begin the reclamation of our inner life: take a flying leap away from double-mindedness and onto Sophia-Christ, 'in whom are hidden all the treasures of wisdom and knowledge' (Colossians 2.3). In practice 'the leap' means placing all that you are discovering about yourself into all that you are discovering about Christ. Next, burn all your boats and blow up all your bridges, which still provide a way of retreat from Christ back to the old indecisiveness. Now proceed with your relationship with him by practising two attitudes: simplicity and transparency. Keep it simple (uncomplicated) and keep it open (no hypocrisy). The heart will find its rest within this relationship: authentic joy will flow as a consequence.

'The cheerful heart has a continual feast' (Proverbs 15.15)

A truly 'cheerful heart' (another translation is 'good morale') has an inner energy which cannot be stopped by accident or change, hence 'continual'. This indomitable quality is stated even in the face of life's cruelty. This person overcomes with courage and self-respect which even poverty cannot drag down.

Still the question persists, how do we come by a 'cheerful heart'? For that we must gather up our 'wisdom' teachings and take them into Sophia-Christ and the New Testament, which teems and glows with joy, summed up in the phrase, 'joy in the Lord', which is rooted in the gospel. To enter into the joy of the Lord we come by way of the main doctrines of the faith – all of which flow out of the character of God the Father. The heart can be 'happy, cheerful' when convinced of the Father's providential and individual care for each of us. Our hope is built upon the unchanging covenant love of 'Abba, Father', revealed in his son Jesus. Reconciled to the Father, our every need becomes his personal concern; we do not trust in a cosmic process but in the Father's plans of love for his children. Notice how, in the Gospels, Jesus never stayed around to unravel or vindicate the Father's actions (see Matthew 6.25–34). Stronger than all the riddles and questions, the paradoxes and anxieties that trouble our lives, is our relationship with God as Abba Father. Jesus lived by that faith unconditionally, which will be enough for us. Hence he could approach the abysmal horrors of the crucifixion 'for the joy set before him' (Hebrews 12.2): the joy of knowing it was the will of his Father.

The New Testament erupts with the joy of the prodigal returned home with the Father and seated at his table. Because of this immense reason for joy, the scriptures do that seemingly impossible thing and *command* God's believing people to rejoice as the only reasonable response to the love of the Father, the Son and the Holy Spirit: 'Be joyful always, pray continually; give thanks in all circumstances, for this is God's will for you in Christ Jesus' (1 Thessalonians 5.16–18). Jesus said: 'I have told you this so that my joy may be in you and that your joy may be complete' (John 15.11).

The way towards the happy heart, manifested in well-being and the cheerful face, is clear: 'Let the word of Christ dwell in you richly as you teach and admonish one another with all wisdom, and as you sing psalms, hymns and spiritual songs with gratitude in your hearts to God' (Colossians 3.16–17). More than any other single thing, praise is the discipline which, year in and year out, grounds the heart and the mind in the joy of the Lord.

Taking it further

Quite deliberately set out to practise joy, practise the happy heart. Gather into a notebook scriptures and other helpful writings that celebrate the happiness of life in God. Make them a regular source of meditation; become so familiar with them that your thought invades your feelings.

> *Be merry, really merry. The life of a true Christian should be a perpetual jubilee, a prelude to the festivals of eternity.*
>
> (St Theophane Venard)

CHAPTER 10

The Vivacious Playmate

Wisdom's people love her because she is beautiful, and because God loves her, and because she bestows joy. In the previous chapter we saw how she brings lovely lines to the cheerful face of the person with a glad heart; now we move on to consider Sophia-Christ's role in creation. She speaks:

> The LORD created me the beginning of his works,
> before all else that he made, long ago.
> Alone, I was fashioned in times long past,
> at the beginning, long before the earth itself.
> When there was yet no ocean I was born,
> no springs brimming with water.
> Before the mountains were settled in their place,
> long before the hills I was born,
> when as yet he had made neither land nor lake
> nor the first clod of earth.
> When he set the heavens in their place I was there,
> when he girdled the earth with the horizon,
> when he fixed the canopy of clouds overhead
> and set the springs of ocean firm in their place,
> when he prescribed its limits for the sea
> and knit together earth's foundations.
> Then I was at his side each day,
> his darling and delight,
> playing in his presence continually,
> playing on the earth, when he had finished it,
> while my delight was in mankind.
>
> (Proverbs 8.22–31, NEB)

Considerable scholarly discussion surrounds the exact form of the word translated here as 'his darling' (8.30). Other versions, including the NIV, give 'craftsman' or 'architect-master craftsman'. But the passage concerns Wisdom's origins and goes on to the enchanting image of her sporting and laughing in the playground of the world (8.30–31), which sounds like the behaviour of a high-spirited youngster rather than that of a senior works manager.

There is a touch of paradise to the scene, a time when 'playing in God's presence' and 'playing on the earth' did not involve a contradiction. William McKane comments, 'Wisdom is a child without a care, her brow unfurrowed by anxiety, the vivacious playmate of God and man, with heaven and earth her playground.'[1] Halfway between heaven and earth, between God and man, exulting in the presence of both, Wisdom's role in creation is to engage the Father and humankind in her joy and delight in existence. This was before Adam's hooligan children vandalized the playground and broke God's windows, nevertheless the vision stands. What is the purpose of Christ's redeeming work? To get the game under way again. The life of our churches, as well as our personal Christian lives, should manifest the good news that in Sophia-Christ the playground is open for business.

Look once more at the scene where the child-wisdom 'was at his side each day'. What did the Father and child speak about, and what was it that gave them such pleasure as they brought the world and humankind out of chaos into existence? Together they pour out onto creation a certain empowerment, a gift, which draws humankind into their game. For it is a wonderful game – not a joke, but a game. Did Jesus have that scene in mind when he chose a child to model the entrance into the kingdom (Matthew 18.1–5)? Children go through their days happily convinced that the whole point and purpose of the project is play.

So what was that original game? Perhaps it was the gift of *imagination*, the magical quality that transforms the flat, rigid dullness of life into a game of limitless possibilities, a dance, a drama of as many acts as you wish. Thomas Howard writes that imagination is 'the faculty by which we suppose correspondences among all things and hence see them as images of one another. It is *image*-ination, the image making faculty.'[2] The image-ing power is not a flight into fancy but Wisdom's gift by which we fly towards actuality. It is as though God first heaped his gifts and blessings on humankind and then Wisdom poured in the ability to imagine these gifts from countless angles.

Samuel Taylor Coleridge, who was brilliantly fascinated by the imagination all his life, suggested that the ability to imagine is the most divine feature of our being: 'it is a dim analogue of creation'. In fact we can hardly put a couple of sentences together (unless we are determined to make them deadly dull) without resort to our image-making instinct through a figure of speech, a metaphor, an analogy or even a parable. We say about someone that 'he had a face like thunder', evoking a meteorological episode over the North Sea to suggest a highly and perhaps dangerously agitated state of mind. We easily refer to places we have never been to, and things we've never seen ('all the tea in China') to express the priceless value to ourselves of a pet hamster. In today's newspaper a famous conductor describes the poor acoustics at the back of a certain concert hall in London as 'like being kissed over the telephone'; we are delighted with the comparison and get his point immediately and memorably.

Sometimes this instinct for illuminating one thing by linking it with something utterly different can be quite bizarre: thus people may use an exotic and fantastic image ('counting the number of angels dancing on a pin-head') to refer to what is the height of dull, pedantic, legalistic hair-splitting. But just coin the right image and it's as satisfying as hitting a bottle on a wall with a stone from 30 paces. Those who have the image-making capability to a high degree we call poets, but we all have it to some extent, given to us as our entrance ticket to Wisdom's game within the web of meanings, which caused God and man such delight as she spun it out over creation. We have stressed verbal image-ing, but of course the same is true for every expression of the gift in the visual arts, music, drama, but also in personal relationships. In fact it is true in any aspect of our life where we can ask, 'And what would happen if I turned it this way a bit and stood it on its end?'

Our imagination works in response to Wisdom's imagination seen in the way the world is. We have the faculty of image-making so that we can detect and decode what Wisdom is saying from out of the world. Wisdom's game includes the Father, who delights to participate even though for him it involves real risk to his honour as he exposes himself to our powers of imagining. Was that the cause of so much merriment between Wisdom, the Father and humankind as they first played together in the park? Did the Father ask Wisdom, 'How do I look in this parable?' and did Wisdom ask, 'Do you think this aphorism really suits me?'

In a wonderful passage, St Ephrem (fourth century) speaks of God stooping to enter the game, his condescension in entering our image-ing world, allowing himself to be pictured in the terms we find lying around:

> Grace, which bent down its stature to the level of man's
> childishness:
> Although God had nothing common with it,
> he clothed himself with the likeness of man
> in order to bring man to the likeness of himself.
> Do not let your intellect be disturbed by mere names,
> for paradise has simply clothed itself in terms that are
> familiar to you:
> It is not because it is poor that it has put on your
> imagery,
> rather, your nature is far too weak to be able
> to attain its greatness, and its beauties are much
> diminished
> by being depicted in the pale colours that you are
> familiar with.[3]

In his superb figure of speech, Coleridge reflects on how we experience creation's imagination (i.e. Wisdom's imagination in the created order):

For all that meets the bodily sense I deem
Symbolical, one mighty alphabet
For infant minds.[4]

He felt the mystery of the world upon his senses as 'symbolical'. Everything is both itself but also something more than itself, for there is something behind everything in the symbolical creation. Thus symbol, parable, figure of speech, are more than means of expression; it is the way Wisdom creates the world.

Sophia 'whom [God] anointed heir of all things, and through whom he made the universe' (Hebrews 1.2) permeates creation not merely as a dash of colour, or like sugar in a cake-mix (there it is again – to talk of wisdom in-dwelling the world we invoke something as simple as baking!), but as its meaning, its order and navigational intelligence, the rhyme and the reason of things, its power to see things in other ways by the imagination. She is the organizing voice behind the visible creation, so that the world is not dumb but has a message to share with humankind, a hymn to proclaim in praise of the creator.

All you have made will praise you, O LORD.
(Psalm 145.10)

The heavens declare the glory of God;
the skies proclaim the work of his hands.
Day after day they pour forth speech.
(Psalm 19.1–2)

In Wisdom's game, creation is empowered to speak symbolically, and we are empowered (gifted) to discern her speech through the right use of our eyes and ears, at the disposal of our imagination. Wisdom speaks, calls, gestures, touches; at times she knocks us off our feet, from out of the world about us. Creation is neither neutral nor hostile, it is Wisdom's servant. The question is not, 'Does Wisdom call to me?' but, 'Can I stay alert long enough to discern and interpret her approach?' Most of us are practically asleep most of the time and plod doggedly on complaining that 'the Lord never speaks to me', which was exactly Job's argument with God.

When at last God does answer Job (see Job 38—42) he does so through his creatures. What happened next is of enormous importance to our understanding of Wisdom's call to us in our daily lives. In fact God doesn't answer Job, handing that task over to his servant creation, confident that his creatures are empowered to witness to Job. The issue for Job was the reality, or otherwise, of God's providential love and care, and as the carnival of creation parades past him each creature speaks symbolically. Everything is there: the sky, sea, mountains, sunrise and darkness, storms, frost, snow, the lioness and her cubs, the mountain goat and the daft ostrich. Everything, by being true to itself, also points to the nature of the providential creator. What was required of Job was that his imagination, served by his eyes and ears, should respond to Wisdom's imagination in a symbolic creation.

Symbolic, but also sacramental. Wisdom has set us in a sacramental creation. Symbols teach – they are indeed a 'mighty alphabet for infant minds' – but a sacrament not only teaches but communicates the Lord of whom it speaks. Bread and wine are symbols of Christ but by faith they are also a means through which Christ comes to nourish our lives. We will settle for one example: the episode of Moses' encounter with God at the burning bush. The writer of the Jewish second book of Esdras (3.19) expresses the symbolic and the sacramental nature of such moments like this: 'Lord, your glory passed through the four gates of fire and earthquake and wind and ice, to give the law to the descendants of Jacob.'

The phenomenon of fire, earthquake, wind and ice are not God, nor are they the glory of God, but in a symbolic and sacramental world they serve God as 'gates' through which he comes to his people.

Look around you at Wisdom's game (image-making, symbolical, sacramental) and take to heart Emily Dickinson's great aphorism:

Not 'Revelation' – 'tis – that waits,
But our unfurnished eyes.[5]

Taking it further

With Wisdom's game in mind, look at the patterns, places and people that make up your life. Are you happy with the way things are? Are some too rigid, dry, dull, lacking life? Does it have to be this way? Now re-imagine those situations and relationships revitalized by Jesus, the 'vivacious playmate'. Now what might they look like? Imagine the best you can, then turn it into prayer for real change.

CHAPTER 11

Ask the Loveliness

Montezuma and his Aztecs looked at the earth and sky and felt inspired to ritual mass-murder. Our modern atheist looks at the world and sees a chance concatenation of physical events with nothing 'behind' it. When Israel's wisdom teachers looked at nature they started with the revelation of the one God who creates for the sheer joy of it, a vision exquisitely caught by the image of the wisdom-child, that 'vivacious playmate', skylarking with men in the playground of the world (Proverbs 8.30–31).

The Teachers contemplated the world and saw not merely a static organism, a neutral platform on which the drama of history is enacted, but creation itself as a major performer in the drama. Wisdom empowers and directs this haunting and mysteriously beautiful world, and calls to man from out of it. Augustine invites us to:

> Ask the loveliness of the earth, ask the loveliness of the sea, ask the loveliness of the wide airy spaces, ask the loveliness of the sky; ask the order of the stars, ask the sun making the daylight with its beams, ask the moon tempering the darkness of the night that follows; ask the living things which move in the waters, which tarry on the land, which fly in the air; ask the souls that are hidden, the bodies that are perceptive, the visible things which must be governed, the invisible things which govern – ask all these things and they will all answer you, 'Look, see we are lovely.' Their loveliness is their confession. And these lovely but mutable things, who has made them, save beauty immutable?[1]

Sophia's loveliness seems to turn towards us; she beckons to us, inviting us to become her partner. Thus the wisdom writings, the seed-bed of Jesus' own thought, (including the closely related Jewish books of Sirach and Wisdom of Solomon) are permeated with instruction on how to respond to Wisdom's love.

> Do not forsake wisdom, and she will protect you;
> love her, and she will watch over you . . .
> Esteem her, and she will exalt you;
> embrace her, and she will honour you.
>
> (Proverbs 4.6, 8)

In words and ideas which pre-vision Christ's relationship with his followers in the Gospels, Wisdom and people commit to one another in love. Love alone is the key to Wisdom's riches. It is futile to attempt to seize hold of her by the throat until she yields up her secrets – an approach that might work if learning motorcycle maintenance, but never with Wisdom. We will come to her as a lover or not at all and the person who loves her will seek her unceasingly.

> Put your feet in wisdom's fetters,
> and your neck into her collar.
> Stoop to carry her on your shoulders,
> and do not chafe at her bonds.
> Come to her whole-heartedly,
> and keep to her ways with all your might.
> Follow her track and she will make herself
> known to you;
> once you have grasped her, never let her go.
> In the end you will find the relief she offers;
> she will transform herself into joy for you.
> Her fetters will become your strong defence,
> and her collar a gorgeous robe.
> Her yoke is a golden ornament,
> and her bonds a purple cord.
> You shall put her on like a gorgeous robe,
> and wear her like a splendid crown.
>
> (Sirach 6.24–31)

If we are serious about Wisdom, an attitude of cool detachment is out of the question; rather the total commitment of love is demanded before she will open to us. The Teacher's language can be sensual (particularly in Proverbs 1—9) and extreme, not a bit like our normal approach to the sermon on a Sunday morning:

> Happy the man who fixes his thought on
>   wisdom
> and uses his brains to think,
> the man who contemplates her ways
> and ponders her secrets.
> Stalk her like a hunter
> and lie in wait beside her path!
> The man who peers in at her windows
> and listens at her keyhole,
> who camps beside her house,
> driving his tent peg into her wall,
> who pitches his tent close by her,
> where it is best for men to live –
> he will put his children in her shade
> and camp beneath her branches,
> sheltered by her from the heat
> and dwelling in the light of her presence.
>
> (Sirach 14.20–27)

The Wisdom-seeker behaves like a stalker, a hunter, a voyeur at her window; he listens for her every noise, he harasses her, he scribbles down and memorizes her every word.

At this point we remind ourselves that the seeker's obsession with Wisdom is about delight in existence. Wisdom is the voice of life in its fullness. The divine mystery of life in the world seeks us before we seek it; or rather we seek it because it first seeks us. The writers are excited by a sense of Wisdom coming towards them as they ponder the world; and they react by running towards her. She is life and the way to life, and the way of life.

> Wisdom shines bright and never fades;
> she is easily discerned by those who love her,
> and by those who seek her she is found.
> She is quick to make herself known to those who desire knowledge of her;
> the man who rises early in search of her will not grow weary in the quest,
> for he will find her seated at his door.
> To set all one's thoughts on her is prudence in its perfect shape,
> and to lie wakeful in her cause is the short way to peace of mind.
> For she herself ranges in search of those who are worthy of her;
> on her daily path she appears to them with kindly intent,
> and in all their purposes meets them half-way.
> (Wisdom 6.12–16)

As she woos men, Wisdom makes an offer which includes everything that people alone in the world might require: wealth and honour (Proverbs 8.18, 21); guidance and security in life (Proverbs 1.33; 2.9); knowledge of God and rest for the soul (Proverbs 2.5).

> To love her is to love life,
> to rise early for her sake is to be filled with joy . . .
> To serve her is to serve the Holy One,
> and the Lord loves those who love her . . .
> If a man trusts her he will possess her.
> (Sirach 4.12–16)

Clearly 'wisdom' is more than a code of conduct with boxes to tick as we 'complete' each one. Many of us have tried that sort of thing and found it a mechanical, chilly process, which seems to end in a glow of self-righteousness. The Teachers do indeed give advice on the business of practical living, for wisdom would be of little interest if it wasn't practical in its effects. Thus we are supplied lights along the edge of the road to prevent us from falling into the ditch. There is advice on bringing up children and the very topical issue of 'to whack or not to whack?'

> Train a child in the way he should go,
> and when he is old he will not turn from it.
> (Proverbs 22.6)

There is shrewd observation on human behaviour:

> An honest answer is like a kiss on the lips.
> (Proverbs 24.6)

We are given serious political maxims:

> Like a muddied spring or a polluted well
> is a righteous man who gives way to the wicked.
> (Proverbs 25.26)

And the not-so-serious domestic comments:

> Better to live on a corner of the roof
> than share a house with a quarrelsome wife.
> (Proverbs 21.9)

Also solemn words about injustice:

> He who oppresses the poor shows contempt for their Maker.
> (Proverbs 41.31)

And about the state of the nation:

> Where there is no revelation, the people cast off restraint;
> but blessed is he who keeps the law.
> (Proverbs 29.18)

But wisdom is more than the sum of its maxims, just as a fire is more than the sum of its sparks. The Teachers will not allow us to make off with the maxims and use them in isolation from the one who is the mysterious, creative Wisdom of the world. They insist on the primacy of love for her and then obedience to the maxims as an expression of that love. Taken forward to its realization and expansion in the person of Jesus, Sophia-Christ, who 'is before all things, and in him all things hold together' (Colossians 1.17), we see God's wisdom at work mending his sin-damaged creation. In Chapter 13 we shall consider how the cross of Christ is the saving wisdom of God, but for the moment we stay with the earthy realism of his teaching. Jesus did not arrive for his mission with a set of parables tailor-made in heaven for speaking about heaven. Rather he pays the most stupendous compliment to ordinary nature, and to people's ordinary lives, by finding his teaching aids ready-made in their world. He could do so because of the intrinsic affinity between the kingdom of God and the processes of the natural world, and of people in their daily lives. He healed the split between the sacred and the profane.

Thus to convey the providential care of the Father we have no need to climb to heaven, but just 'consider the ravens . . . ' (see Luke 12.24–28). Wisdom insists that nature and supernature belong together in one order. Every 'natural' thing is also spiritual in this symbolic and sacramental creation. What this can mean for the way we lead our lives is wonderfully suggested by Francis of Assisi, one of Sophia's special children. His ecstatic love for God encountered in the mystery of the world was incomparably sketched by G. K. Chesterton, who described Francis as:

> this amazingly unworldly and almost maddening single-minded infant . . . the detail over which his monks went mad with joy was the universe itself; the only thing really worthy of enjoyment . . . Francis always assumed that everyone must be just as anxious about their common relative, the water rat, as he was. He planned a visit to the Emperor to draw his attention to the needs of 'his little sisters the larks'. He used to talk to any thieves and robbers he met about their misfortune in being unable to give rein to their desire for holiness

> . . . He expressed in loftier and bolder language than any earthly thinker the conception that laughter is as divine as tears. He called his monks the mountebanks of God. He never forgot to take pleasure in a bird as it flashed past him, or a drop of water as it fell from his finger: he was, perhaps, the happiest of the sons of man . . . he named the fire 'brother' and the water 'sister' . . . he appealed in the sermon to the fishes 'that they alone were saved in the Flood' . . . He could not see why he should not be on good terms with all things . . . His questions were blasting and devastating, like the questions of a child . . . To him the world was small, not because he had any views as to its size, but for the reason that gossiping ladies find it small, because so many relatives were to be found in it. If you had taken him to the loneliest star the madness of an astronomer can conceive, he would only have beheld in it the features of a new friend.[2]

It only remains to make an obvious connection between our readings of the old Teachers and Francis. For all their vast differences, both pursued the primacy of love for the God who comes to us out of creation. First comes love, then understanding and holiness. First love, then Wisdom's self-revelation. First love, then will follow praise and service to God, reverential awe before the almighty Lord, and obedience to him. Without love in the ascendancy knowledge can be dangerous stuff ('Where is the wisdom we have lost in knowledge?' – p. 7), for then the powers of love immanent in the world are overwhelmed by market forces, technology and a dubious 'progress'. The result is a heartless drive for productivity with power and the profit margin the sole criteria. But the old writers, in common with Francis demonstrated the reality that Wisdom reveals herself to those who will love her. Jesus said: 'If anyone loves me, he will obey my teaching. My Father will love him, and we will come to him and make our home with him' (John 14.23).

Taking it further

'Taking it further' means taking it into oneself and being changed by it. Look through the chapter once more and list three insights for reflection and action. Tim Hansel warns against the dangers of inaction: 'We don't need fasten-your-seatbelts signs in our pews because we no longer fly. We're like a group of geese attending meetings every Sunday where we talk passionately about flying and then get up and walk home.'[3]

CHAPTER 12

Kingdom Wisdom

It is a wide and generous wisdom that can enter the mind of the doubter, the cynic, the hedonist, and even of the unbeliever. We need to listen sympathetically to their struggles with faith and then to articulate them to others. Koheleth is our man. And it is worth mentioning once again that the daring Koheleth, astute world watcher, was part of Jesus' own formation in wisdom. The following is typical of his thought as a 'vicarious doubter':

> No-one can comprehend what goes on under the sun. Despite all his efforts to search it out, man cannot discover its meaning. Even if a wise man claims he knows, he cannot really comprehend it . . . All share a common destiny – the righteous and the wicked, the good and the bad, the clean and the unclean, those who offer sacrifices and those who do not . . . Enjoy life with your wife, whom you love, and all the days of this meaningless life that God has given you under the sun – all your meaningless days.
>
> (Ecclesiastes 8.17; 9.2, 9)

That looks and sounds remarkably familiar. I think I read something like it in last weekend's glossy supplement. A simple philosophy of 'keep your head down, enjoy the moment, try to make the best of the hand fate has dealt you because there's nothing out there, or up there, to help you'. But behind Koheleth's words from within the skin of people adrift in their spiritual confusion, quietly despairing of ever making much sense of it all, exists everyone's great question: 'Is this a good or bad world?' It is a reasonable test of any claim to serious wisdom that it should cast some light on our question.

Otherwise we have no clue to the nature of our world-home (is it a good or an evil place?). We are cruelly deceived by our times of happiness and optimism if all the while they occur within the barbed-wire perimeter fence of an unjust, merciless world. Likewise, we shouldn't be unduly weighed down in our low times if in fact they occur within a fundamentally just and hopeful creation.

Chesterton, once more, writing on the austere personal disciplines of Francis and his monks:

> We look at the rise of Christianity and conceive it as a rise of self-abnegation, and almost of pessimism. It does not occur to us that the mere assertion that this raging and confounding universe is governed by justice and mercy is a piece of staggering optimism fit to set all men capering.[1]

If we could look this world full in the face and assert that justice and mercy hold sway, at once all the lights would come on. Then history, and our personal stories within its drama, proceed against the backdrop of a universe illuminated by hope. But where that conviction is missing all we can do is live out our time here as ingeniously and as bravely as we can, against a dark background and in the sort of stoical atmosphere sketched by Koheleth. Small wonder, then, that so much of our merry-making and 'entertainments' are more than a touch desperate. The multi-channel selector is probably the iconic piece of equipment that will suggest to archaeologists in a thousand years' time just how unhappy we were, once we switched everything off and sat alone in the dark. Once the images stop flickering we are returned to our feeling of loneliness within a dark world. What about the iconic celebration? That must be our amazing firework displays, where our technology is pitted against the night sky in a defiant refusal to allow empty darkness the last word. But it takes more than a few sparklers, or even a truckload of them, to answer that question of ours: 'This place, is it good or evil?'

Wisdom cuts across our inconclusive wanderings. She speaks:

> Love and faithfulness meet together;
> righteousness and peace kiss each other.
> (Psalm 85.10)

The inspiration for this 'staggering optimism' was Israel's emancipation from her 70-year captivity in Babylon. God is praised for keeping his ancient covenant pledge to his people. The words are established upon God's saving action, his kingly reign. 'Love' translates the beautiful Hebrew word *hesed*, meaning strong loyalty in love, by which God willingly binds and commits himself to keep his promises. He is that sort of God, honour-bound because he is covenant-bound to uphold his world in 'righteousness and peace'. Thus Israel's return from exile was a sign that God is to be trusted in the way he handles nations. 'Righteousness' (his saving love) and the blessings of his 'peace' have met and kissed, uniting at the point where God's love prevails.

That saving event, in itself a relatively small, localized episode in the violent affairs of the ancient world, serves like a transparent slide. Placed within the 'projector' of inspired prophetic vision its symbolic picture (symbolic of God's practical rules in men's affairs) is thrown forward, enlarged, to be fulfilled in the person and work of Jesus, the divine wisdom. Therefore Wisdom is not merely a commentator, a lecturer or an adviser, but a doer, a maker and a mender, bestowing the life and blessing of which she speaks. In Christ, Sophia's talk of love and faithfulness, righteousness and peace coming together in the world are translated into action. Because of Christ these words describe God's way of governing creation. Christ's work was the decisive act of 'release from exile' for captives. He announced the commencement of his ministry by the following words: 'Jesus went into Galilee, proclaiming the good news of God. "The time has come," he said, "The kingdom of God is near. Repent and believe the good news!"' (Mark 1.14–15).

With the coming of Jesus, the longed-for reign of God is invading the world, news 'fit to set all men capering' for it guarantees the safe keeping of the world within God's care. Everything we read of Jesus, who he is and what he did, are designed to convince us of God's fatherly rule. Jesus, God's wisdom, proclaimed God's authority and by his achievements made it reality. His Jewish listeners understood the term 'kingdom of God' in the Old Testament sense, not as a territory but as a condition of blessing due to God's kingly power and compassion. Thus his reign is neither a spatial of static concept, but a dynamic concept, the rule of God in action. It is therefore intimately tied up with Christ's own person and his ministry. By his presence, through his words and works, the kingdom of God is 'happening', invading his contemporaries' world. Because he was in their midst, the kingdom was in their midst (Luke 17.21); because he is near to them, the kingdom is near to them (Mark 1.14–15).

In the Old Testament and in the Israel of Jesus' time, the reign of God was understood as God's practical protection for the helpless, the weak, the poor, the blind and the leper, the widow and the orphan (Isaiah 35.3–7). The Gospels are therefore making a stupendous claim when they put together a free combination of quotations from the Isaiah passages (Isaiah 29.18; 61.1–3) and apply them directly to Jesus as the one who fulfils them both literally and physically, and also interprets them as symbols of spiritual disorders (Luke 7.21–22; Matthew 11.4–6). Thus the disciples are sent out to 'preach the message: The kingdom of heaven is near.' How near? As close as Jesus is to them, for he is the kingdom, he is the king-in-action. At the same time, the disciples were to enact, demonstrate, make-happen the substance of the message as they 'heal the sick, raise the dead, cleanse those who have leprosy and [the spiritual component] drive out demons' (Matthew 10.8).

Thus we learn that our need is not simply a question of lack of essentials or substandard essentials (education, medicine, employment, housing, etc.), but of an oppressive, occupying, demonic power. Jesus did not come merely to problem-solve, to respond to our felt needs, but to reach beyond and behind them, to engage with and break the satanic hold. He traces human feebleness further and further back, to where we are enmeshed in our guilty past (like a swimmer entangled in rigging of a sunken ship) and there he cuts the cords by the power of his cross and resurrection. Christ is the redemptive and redeeming wisdom of God who came among us to expel the enemy power squatting on his Father's territory. Evil is not a 'problem' but an enemy to be overcome. By his healing miracles, as well as by his 'nature' miracles (e.g. stilling the storm) Sophia-Christ affirmed creation as 'good'; 'the kingdom of God is near', and here are the signs and the evidence. Thus in Christ the creation and the new creation are linked, a truth powerfully expressed when he deliberately healed the sick on the Sabbath:

> So, because Jesus was doing these things on the Sabbath, the Jews persecuted him. Jesus said to them, 'My Father is always at his work to this very day, and I, too, am working.' For this reason the Jews tried all the harder to kill him; not only was he breaking the Sabbath, but he was even calling God his own Father, making himself equal with God.
>
> Jesus gave them this answer: 'I tell you the truth, the Son can do nothing by himself; he can only do what he sees his Father doing, for whatever the Father does the Son also does. For the Father loves the Son and shows him all he does. Yes, to your amazement he will show you even greater things than these.'
>
> (John 5.16–20)

In scripture the Sabbath is the sign of creation (Genesis 2.2) and of the Exodus (Deuteronomy 5.15). That is, man can rest because God has completed his work of creation and of new creation. In his Sabbath healings Jesus claimed Lordship over 'all things', visible and invisible. In so doing he announced the full realization of Wisdom's immense claim:

> Love and faithfulness meet together;
> righteousness and peace kiss each other.
>
> (Psalm 85.10)

It is upon this foundation that the 'staggering optimism' of our assertion that 'this raging and confounding universe is governed by justice and mercy' is established.

How is Wisdom 'proved right' by all her children in this claim? In a word, by doing justice and mercy wherever we are placed. Here are a couple of simple examples. A Muslim Pakistani taxi driver in Rotherham was startled to see a group of people with buckets surround his car. They insisted on washing his screen, not for money but, as they explained, because they were Christians and they just wanted to do this small thing for him out of respect and love. He told them he had been many years in England and this was the first time a Christian had done anything for him. Young people from another church met for prayer on a Saturday morning before going off with their brooms to sweep the streets of the parish, for love of God and of people. Such joyful serving, which demonstrates the kingdom, will soon have started parishioners asking, 'Why?'

In his practice of the presence of the kingdom Jesus did two seemingly contradictory things for people. He rooted them and then he uprooted them. Human beings need proper rooting (God 'rooted' Adam in Eden). We need security, nourishment, justice, clean water, etc. Children cannot grow straight unless rooted in sound conditions. Wisdom's children will therefore do whatever they can to support 'rooting' enterprises. But at the same time the kingdom gospel calls on everyone to 'uproot' from overmuch comfort which can encircle the life and hold it in bondage to self-centredness. Uproot and be ready and available to follow the Lord wherever he leads. Here lies the tension and the apparent paradox of the kingdom. One of Wisdom's children's tasks is to appraise the wisdom of their church and see how successfully it holds both rooting and uprooting in creative tension.

Taking it further

Can we assume that your church is committed to demonstrating the reality of the kingdom, seen in the pursuit of mercy and justice? This is sometimes called witnessing by 'presence'. Within such a context of love, friendship and integrity, 'proclamation' becomes possible. Without that context, speaking of

God's reign is quite unreal, a disembodied, wordy activity that connects with nothing in the lives of local people. With other concerned people in your church, review the quality of kingdom 'presence' in your locality and the penetration of kingdom 'proclamation'.

CHAPTER 13

The Wisdom of the Cross

What should a market-savvy communicator do when his core message repels the public? Sugar-coat it, soft-pedal the controversial stuff, 're-package', allow the considerations of 'relevance' to be his guide? Not when he is utterly convinced of the integrity of his message. The apostle Paul refused to budge an inch on the primacy of substance over style: 'we preach Christ crucified . . . Christ the power of God and the wisdom of God' (1 Corinthians 1.23–24). In that same passage Paul acknowledges that the cross places the gospel into headlong conflict with the various spiritualities and philosophies of that world. But they are only ideas and squiggles on paper – brilliant words and squiggles maybe, but the message of the cross is of a different order. It is an act of stupendous power, something which we use words to describe, but the gospel is in the fact of the act of the cross. Cardinal Newman warned against what he called 'shedding the riches and vitality of actual experience in order to promote artificial clarity'.[1] The world is saved by the 'riches and vitality' of the crucified Christ and Paul will never tamper with that truth for the sake of a dubious 'relevance'.

Yet the cross is a tough message. The idea that God's saving wisdom should have come in the person of a mutilated Jewish manual worker provoked outrage and derision, an insuperable offence to Jews and madness to the 'Greek' mind. Various influences, threats, bribes and compromises were attempting to shift the Church away from its cross-centred vision and on to more 'reasonable' and culturally acceptable aspects of Christ's message. But Paul would have none of it: 'if we or an angel from heaven should preach a gospel other than the one we preached to you, let him be eternally condemned!' (literally 'anathema') (Galatians 1.8–9). Paul knew full well what he was doing. Rather than go with the cultural grain and seek to negotiate a peaceful co-existence with the other 'wisdoms' on offer, he deliberately set out to provoke confrontation in order to establish the distinctive credentials of Christ the crucified wisdom of God.

At least the Christian evangelists had no need to explain in detail the processes of a crucifixion to their hearers, since it was a horribly familiar spectacle. For the authorities it was a low-cost, highly effective deterrent to criminal behaviour, rebellious slaves or anti-government activists. Designed not only to kill, a crucifixion obliterated the victim, slowly, in public. All the ingenuity of an executioner's sadism had free rein, and the bodies were then commonly left exposed for scavenging birds and wild animals to devour. When Paul spoke of 'Christ crucified' every listener in the Greek-speaking East understood that this Christ had suffered the most appalling death. The educated listener must inevitably have thought that the Christian claims that the crucified Christ is God's son, the divine wisdom incarnate, Lord of heaven and earth and judge of the world, were lunacy – disgusting, repellent lunacy. As Martin Hengel writes, 'The enemies of Christianity always referred to the disgracefulness of the death of Jesus with great emphasis and malicious pleasure. A god or son of God dying on a cross! That was enough to put paid to the new religion!'[2] That is, unless you were yourself on the receiving end of cruelty and oppression, in which case the announcement that almighty God had joined the poor at the point of the most appalling expression of man's cruelty to man, crucifixion, will have seemed astoundingly wonderful news. But the general contempt for the crucified Jesus and his followers is illustrated by a well-known example of early graffiti: a crucified figure with a donkey's head is being reverenced by a young man, with the Greek inscription, 'Alexamenos worships God'.

In 4 BC 2,000 Jewish prisoners were crucified around Jerusalem, and again, in the year of terror, AD 70, there was another holocaust with mass executions. Yet the cross was never accepted within Judaism as a symbol of Jewish martyrdom, since Deuteronomy 21.23 made that connection unthinkable: 'Anyone who is hung on a tree is under God's curse'. On those scriptural grounds Paul, before his conversion, hounded the memory of Jesus of Nazareth, in the form of the young Church, because Christ crucified meant Christ accursed by God. His encounter with the risen Jesus on the Damascus road (Acts 9.1–5) blew apart his neat theological equation: Christ on the cross = Christ cursed by God. How could that be, if Christ was speaking to him from heaven's glory (and with extraordinary tenderness)? The answer dawned on him with two words: it was 'for me', or 'for us'. Everything Paul had said about the crucifixion he continued to say, but now with the transforming thrust of those two astonishing words: 'Christ redeemed us from the curse of the law by becoming a curse *for us.* For it is written, "Cursed is everyone who is hung on a tree"' (Galatians 3.13). In fact those solemn words 'becoming a curse for us' are a circumlocution, a roundabout way of expressing an even more staggering meaning: 'God made Christ a cursed one for our sakes.'

The 'wisdom of the cross' provides two measurements without which it isn't possible to live a truly human life. First, it measures, weighs and places a price on the reality of human sin and guilt before God. What must be the truth about my spiritual condition if it required the sinless son of God, the Lord of love, to be 'made a cursed one' for my healing? 'God made him who had no sin to be sin for us, so that in him we might become the righteousness of God' (2 Corinthians 5.21). And the second measurement revealed in the cross concerns the love of God. The trajectory of that love is traced in an early church hymn (Philippians 2.5–11) in which Christ 'empties himself' of everything that could prevent him from coming into the full realization of our humanity. His love moves, travels, transforms itself into 'the form of a servant', for our sakes going all the way to 'the death on the cross'. The cross settles every question about the trustworthiness and resilience of God's love for us. An invincible logic derives from the crucified Christ. 'He who did spare his own Son, but gave him up for us all – how will he not also, along with him, graciously give us all things?' (Romans 8.32). The generous friend who bailed you out to the tune of five million pounds will not quibble over an extra ten pence.

'For me' – 'For us' became the spearhead of Paul's evangelism and the core of his personal existence: 'I live by faith in the Son of God, who loved me and gave himself *for me*' (Galatians 2.20). With his imagination on fire with the mystery of Christ's saving love for the world, it is small wonder that he found powerful images by which to express it. One particularly striking picture illustrating how Christ received our death penalty into his own body is given in Colossians 2.13–14: 'God . . . forgave us all our sins, having cancelled the written code, with its regulations, that was against us and that stood opposed to us; he took it away, nailing it to the Cross.' In another translation: 'God has cancelled the writ issued against us, which enumerated the statutes we had violated, and destroyed it by nailing it to the cross.'

Now imagine Jesus on his way to crucifixion, carrying the beam of the cross on his shoulder. Slung around his neck is the board – the titulus – on which is detailed the crime deemed to merit crucifixion: 'Jesus of Nazareth, King of the Jews'. That board was nailed up over his head as he hung on the cross (see John 19.17–22). Paul is saying, 'As you watch him there, can't you see what is happening? The hand of God reaches in and rips off that board, and in its place he nails up another statement, which is the true reason for his death: "The writ issued against us".' It is God's rightful claim on our lives – in fact it is the unfulfilled IOU we each of us carry around through life. It is the statement of our obligation to love God above all and our neighbour as ourselves.

If you come near enough to the cross you will be able to make out, in the closely written lines on the board, details of your own debt of love to God and to neighbour. At this point you might pause to ask how the other various 'wisdoms' in vogue in our society deal with the fact of personal sin. The answer is, in various ways, the simplest and least demanding of which is to deny the existence of any such IOU. Or to attempt to pay it off in the future by improved behaviour (this way turns us into Pharisees); or to go through life never quite sure if you have done enough to atone for sins (this way turns us into religious neurotics); or to abandon the whole project because who can ever know when you have done enough? (this way lies cynicism and the non-committal shrug of indifference).

The 'wisdom of the cross', the secret of a renewed and cleansed conscience at peace with God, is to see that every outstanding claim in your IOU, every sin (past, present and even future) mentioned there over Christ's wounded head, God has erased, cancelled, written 'paid in full' across it. And the simple intention of evangelism is to invite our friends to come close enough to the cross to see that their debt is paid also. God's holy love is astonishing: it will forgive anything, but it overlooks nothing.

Such is the wisdom of the cross that it goes on to deal with the supernatural powers that batten-down on human existence, a condition we all experience but find almost impossible to define. Paul continues in Colossians 2.15: 'And having disarmed the powers and authorities he made a public spectacle of them, triumphing over them by the cross.'

The 'powers and authorities' are agents of the one satanic power that Jesus came to break, they are 'his hordes, those manifold developments and effusions of the spirit of wickedness with their own combination of intelligence and lust for power, they exist by influencing the world and mankind in every sector and at all levels'.[3] Any response to our human condition which doesn't acknowledge and deal with the reality of malign supernatural powers would be hopelessly naive. Wherever human activity and organization opens itself up to Godless ambitions and behaviour it becomes susceptible to demonic infiltration and possession. We have no need to go into the forests to watch the witchdoctor muttering his incantations over a slaughtered chicken to witness 'the powers' at work. They are far more sinister and potent when they come in the shape of smartly dressed individuals with lap-tops and BMWs. They are present wherever arrogance, greed and lust for power colonize the intelligence of institutions – political, commercial, cultural and, yes, religious. At an everyday level we experience those supernatural powers as an ambience which is gloomy, fearful, hostile, hateful, oppressive, pessimistic – in a word, demonic – in which society is compelled to live unless we move into Christ's victory.

Those 'authorities and powers', manipulating the available and willing state and religious bureaucracies, were able to drive Jesus to his death, only to be totally outwitted by the wisdom of the cross. By his death he 'disarmed' them in a stunning reversal: he dragged those powers into the light and ruined them. By the act of removing the alienating barriers of sin and guilt between God and man, and opening up the way of reconciliation in the forgiveness of sins, Christ broke the satanic hold on the race.

So how did the apostle Paul cope with the 'embarrassment' of a crude, brutal, physical cross in his evangelism? He gloried in it! Reminding the Galatian Christians of the effects of his teaching in his mission among them: 'Before your very eyes Jesus Christ was clearly portrayed as crucified' (Galatians 3.1). The word translated here as 'clearly portrayed' is more directly 'placarded'. There exists an example of its use in the literature of that period in which an irate father orders a placard to be set up announcing (pub landlords, bookmakers, credit card agencies, take note!) that he will no longer be responsible for his son's debts. Far from attempting to dilute the culturally awkward matter of 'Christ crucified', Paul thrusts it to the front of his appeal. His language invites the reader to see him hiring the largest and most prominent billboard in the main square, opposite the chief temples and shrines. On it he pastes up one great stark, scandalous image of Christ crucified with the slogan 'The wisdom of God'. Wisdom is cruciform, however much it affronts the sensibilities of a society. Paul made it a challenge to every philosophical and spiritual-religious system, from Orthodox Judaism to the latest chic gnostic sect. He concludes his letter to the Galatians with the manifesto, 'May I never boast except in the cross of our Lord Jesus Christ, through which the world has been crucified to me, and I to the world' (Galatians 6.14). The wisdom of the cross is the measure of all things.

Taking it further

The challenge seems to be this: How can a church 'placard' Christ crucified without being dismissed as repetitive, monotonous and even fanatical? How can we present the stark simplicity of the cross in the colourful intrigue of the parables? How can evangelism sound more like 'wisdom' and less like shouting through a megaphone?

CHAPTER 14

The Wisdom of Following

A young man carrying a bomb under his coat walks into a bar in Jerusalem and blows himself and many others to bits. Whatever we may think of the Islamic person's zeal for their cause or their urge to take the fast track to paradise, their readiness to spend everything for their convictions is a searching challenge to Christians. Suicide and deliberately provoking martyrdom is not our style, though there was a time when the Church took Jesus' words as a call to make ready for martyrdom:

> He then began to teach them that the Son of Man must suffer many things and be rejected by the elders, chief priests and teachers of the law, and that he must be killed and after three days rise again. He spoke plainly about this and Peter took him aside and began to rebuke him . . . Then he called the crowd to him along with his disciples and said: 'If anyone would come after me, he must deny himself and take up his cross and follow me. For whoever wants to save his life will lose it, but whoever loses his life for me and for the gospel will save it.'
>
> (Mark 8.31–35)

The wisdom of the cross holds within it the wisdom of our discipleship: Christ carried his cross for me, I will carry my cross for him. But his cross wasn't a thing of words only; it wasn't merely a metaphor for love of God and people – the world isn't saved or lives mended by the power of a symbol. A figure of speech without the act it figures is empty. We spent the previous chapter pondering the unspeakable brutality of the cross, a barbarous, screaming thing of blood, iron, vinegar and flies.

That was the point of Jesus' exchange with Peter, who couldn't, or wouldn't conceive of real nails and a sharp spearhead tearing into literal soft flesh, membrane and bone. So when in the same breath Jesus speaks of his cross and then of ours, why should we assume that whereas his is real, ours is only a figure of speech? Because in Luke's account Jesus adds the word 'daily' to our cross-bearing: 'he must . . . take up his cross daily' (Luke 9.23). Since it isn't possible to be crucified more than once, 'daily' is directing our attention away from the moment of execution to another aspect of that long walk from Pilate's hall to Golgotha: in fact, to its start.

When a condemned man staggered out into the dazzling Palestinian sunlight carrying the beam of his cross, his first ordeal was to face the mob – hostile, jeering, there to settle old scores or simply to relish the free entertainment. He must make the desolating walk through the crowds on his route, a defenceless target for their ridicule. A rabbinical saying assured the crowds that the spiritual authorities allowed such behaviour: 'Come and hear . . . anyone who strikes a man who is being led out to execution . . . is free of punishment . . . for the victim counts as a dead man.'[1]

The expression 'to carry the cross' refers to a disciple's decision to follow Christ in spite of the opposition of the crowd. In some places, such as the Sudan or Pakistan, that opposition can be severe, violent and even deadly; for ourselves, more commonly we are made to feel odd, excluded, a touch fanatical, guilty of 'taking the moral high ground' and other crimes against secularism. But always there is a cost. Christ separates and divides even in families; he compels people to choose to be for or against him. How mistaken we are to trivialize 'bearing the cross' when we refer to circumstances that test our patience: 'Our new minister has this odd twitching mannerism when he preaches, but that's a cross we shall just have to bear!' Not a bit of it. A scholar writes, 'In the New Testament "to carry the cross" does not mean "self-denial" but actual "self-surrender". It is not a question of self-discipline by self-denial but of an unreserved surrender of one's person.'[2] Of course self-denial is essential to discipleship, but however we understand the term it still leaves my-self in charge to decide how far I want this self-denial business to go. Self-surrender really is radically different and looks something like this:

> O let thy sacred will
> All thy delight in me fulfil!
> Let me not think an action mine own way,
> But as thy love shall sway,
> Resigning up the rudder to thy skill.[3]

Very beautifully the verse identifies the wisdom of self-surrender. According to George Herbert what we are surrendering is our own half-blind, erratic, restless attempts to navigate, and what we receive in its place is the delight of God's will working itself out in our lives, which sounds like a terrific exchange. But how does 'self-surrender' come about while this selfish 'self' is most unwilling to relinquish the driving seat? Jesus surrendered himself, and gave beyond taking back; he was totally committed, but we are made of different stuff. Perhaps the willing and total mutual surrender of two people when they fall in love is a clue. You *fall* for someone, as the saying goes: it is as spontaneous and as uncontrived as falling into a hole in the road on a dark night. And if something of that sort hasn't happened between Jesus and ourselves, to make self-surrender the most obvious and desirable transaction in the world, it is because of one thing: as yet we don't find him sufficiently attractive.

The theme runs throughout the biblical story of the people, their God, and the besetting sin of ingratitude and spiritual infidelity. No wonder Israel's old story was expressed as an on-off-on-off love affair with God, and as a marriage damaged by Israel's flightiness. No chance of an all-consuming self-surrender while the heart wanders as a consequence of ingratitude. For this reason Christ's people come together to share bread and wine, broken and poured out, in obedience to Christ's command that we 'do this in remembrance of me' (see 1 Corinthians 11.23–26). We call to mind what too easily slips out of our mind, namely the price he paid for our salvation. We must learn to gaze on our crucified Lord and to endure his gaze on us. 'Long-looking, long-desiring, long-loving, these win at last to the inmost being of a thing.'[4]

We are suggesting that at the heart of the self-surrender of 'carrying the cross' is contemplation of Christ's cross. There lies the originating power of the holiness which affects every aspect of our personality and behaviour: 'You are not your own; you were bought at a price. Therefore honour God with your body' (1 Corinthians 6.19–20).

Self-consecration is then no longer a desperate wrench of control from the self but a glad, grateful response to our Lord; the very least we can do. The saints have left us their wisdom on how the power of Christ's love turns self-serving people into willing agents of that love. They mention four steps:

Meditation

On the cost to Jesus of his saving death on the cross. Taking a verse or a passage of scripture (see pages 87–90), pondering a picture or an icon, turning the scene over and over in the mind and down into the deepest imagination, which will lead on to the next stage of . . .

Contemplation

Words about Jesus become in our meditating minds images of him, and we 'see' the word. Walking among our pictures, we stay there pondering, wondering and worshipping his unspeakable love. Contemplation leads on to . . .

Jubilation

As we glimpse the astonishing extent of Christ's love for us on the cross, his resurrection and his presence with us by his Holy Spirit, joy is the only possible response; praise is the overflow of our grateful hearts. And jubilation leads on to . . .

Compassion

Is this a surprise? It is the logic of rejoicing in the love of God in Christ's self-sacrifice for us. John says, 'This is how we know what love is: Jesus Christ laid down his life for us. And we ought to lay down our lives for our brothers' (1 John 3.16). Compassion is dynamic and creative, like Christ's compassion for us; by definition it has the power to enter into other people's needs. Scripture concludes that Christ's self-offering for us leads to our self-offering on behalf of others, that he has purchased every inch of our lives, that he changes us from self-regarding takers into self-forgetful givers. Such transformations are contained within his charge to deny ourselves, take up our cross and follow him, and what Herbert called 'resigning up the rudder to thy skill'.

But in all honesty, self-surrender – as opposed to mere self-denial, and in spite of the impact upon us of Jesus' dying love – is for many of us an elusive thing. How often we find ourselves profoundly moved to sincerely want to make a final, conclusive surrender of all that we are and have to the Lord in response to his love, only to fail. Being the people we are we know from long experience that we cannot commit ourselves to the Lord in a super-glue sort of manner, in a once-for-all irrevocable act; we try time and again but it seems never to last. After a while we are taking control back into our own hands. And there lies our problem, with '*our hands*'. With 'our hands' we give and with 'our hands' we take our life away from the Lord again. The secret would seem to be that we need to commit ourselves as far as *his* hands, where they can take over and hold us fast. A tenuous and wobbly commitment it may be, but just enough to get us into the hands which will take over and not let us go as they fashion God's designs in us.

Taking it further

For your meditation → contemplation → jubilation → compassion . . .

> My God, I love thee – not because
> I hope for heaven thereby,
> Nor yet because who love thee not
> Are lost eternally.

Thou, O my Jesus, thou didst me
  Upon the cross embrace;
For me didst bear the nails and spear,
  And manifold disgrace;

And griefs and torments numberless,
  And sweat of agony,
Yea, death itself, and all for one
  Who was thine enemy.

Then why, O blessèd Jesus Christ,
  Should I not love thee well?
Not for the sake of winning heaven,
  Nor of escaping hell;

Not with the hope of gaining aught,
  Not seeking a reward;
But as thyself hast lovèd me,
  O ever-loving Lord!

E'en so I love thee, and will love,
  And in thy praise will sing;
Solely because thou art my God,
  And my eternal King.[5]

Christ's cross

Christ's cross across this face,
across the ear like this,
Christ's cross across this eye.
Christ's cross across this nose.

Christ's cross across this mouth.
Christ's cross across this throat.
Christ's cross across this back.
Christ's cross across this side.

Christ's cross across this stomach,
(like this it is just fine).
Christ's cross across this gut,
Christ's cross across this spine.

Christ's cross across my arms,
from my shoulders to my hands.
Christ's cross across my thighs,
Christ's cross across my legs.

Christ's cross with me before.
Christ's cross with me behind.
Christ's cross against each trouble
both in hillock and in glen.

Christ's cross across my teeth,
lest to me come harm or hurt.
Christ's cross across my stomach.
Christ's cross across my heart.

Christ's cross up to heaven's span.
Christ's cross down to earth.
Let no evil or harm
come to my body or soul.

Christ's cross across my sitting,
Christ's cross across my lying,
Christ's cross my whole power
till we reach heaven's King.

Christ's cross across my church,
across my community.
Christ's cross in the next world.
Christ's cross in the present day.

From the tip of my head
to the nail of my foot,
Christ against each peril,
the shelter of your cross.

Till the day of my death,
before going in this clay,
joyfully I will make
Christ's cross across my face.[6]

Ah, holy Jesus, how hast thou offended,
That man to judge thee hath in hate pretended?
By foes derided, by thine own rejected,
O most afflicted.

Who was the guilty? Who brought this upon thee?
Alas, my treason, Jesus, hath undone thee.
'Twas I, Lord Jesus, I it was denied thee:
I crucified thee.

Lo, the good Shepherd for the sheep is offered:
The slave hath sinnèd, and the Son hath suffered:
For man's atonement, while he nothing heedeth,
God intercedeth.

For me, kind Jesus, was thy incarnation,
Thy mortal sorrow, and thy life's oblation;
Thy death of anguish and thy bitter passion,
For my salvation.

Therefore, kind Jesus, since I cannot pay thee,
I do adore thee, and will ever pray thee,
Think on thy pity and thy love unswerving,
Not my deserving.[7]

CHAPTER 15

The Spirit of Wisdom

It looks like a large brick, weighs as much and makes an excellent doorstop in warm weather. We are, of course, speaking about the *Merck Manual of Diagnostics and Therapy* (14th edition). Its wisdom helped my wife, our own 'health professional', to nurse the family through some tricky episodes in the Far East: 2,500 pages covering every imaginable condition and a good many beyond my imagining. The point of this trivial observation is that Jesus left nothing like a *Merck Manual of Wisdom*, a comprehensive code for every circumstance, arranged from A to Z. In fact when we look in the Gospels it is striking how selective his detailed instructions are. Which raises the question, how can Sophia's children 'prove her right' when they don't know what she wants?

What Jesus has given us in the Gospels is a series of typical kingdom-wisdom events as *examples* and *signs* of what happens when the grace and power of God's reign penetrate the life of this world. They are teachings, healings, actions, reactions and promises that *illustrate* that new life; *symptoms* of the presence of the divine wisdom. Our part is to meditate prayerfully on those signs, illustrations, examples, symptoms and symbols for the wisdom-principles they convey, and then to extend the logic of those principles to illuminate other areas of experience. We are not left to our own devices in this task, as if by our own wit we can decode those events and words in the Gospels. The Holy Spirit, who inspired the Gospel writers to record those episodes, is with us to guide our thinking into wisdom. Hence the mysterious sense of timeliness and modernity when we read the ancient scriptures under the instruction of the Holy Spirit. When 'Wisdom' declares:

> I prayed, and understanding was given me,
> I called on God, and the Spirit of Wisdom came to me.
> (Wisdom 7:7)

we understand that the 'Spirit of Wisdom' is addressing a mind already informed and attuned by God's word. The Spirit who first gave the word of wisdom by inspiration and revelation comes to breathe on that word in our minds, spreading its light and power throughout our inner world.

In a vital passage (1 Corinthians 2.6–10) the apostle Paul claims that we 'speak a message of wisdom among the mature, but not the wisdom of this age or of the rulers of this age, who are coming to nothing. No, we speak of God's secret wisdom, a wisdom that has been hidden' (2.6–7). He then proceeds to describe how that which is inaccessible and unattainable to sinful man, God's secret and hidden wisdom, is actually communicated to us: 'but God has revealed it to us by his Spirit. The Spirit searches all things, even the deep things of God' (2.10). He then gives the example from common experience of our inability to communicate at depth even between ourselves as fellow human beings. 'For who among men knows the thoughts of a man except the spirit within him? In the same way no-one knows the thoughts of God except the Spirit of God' (2.11). There follows, as a consequence of the Holy Spirit releasing light and power from his ancient word, the gift of wisdom. 'We have not received the spirit of the world but the Spirit who is from God, that we may understand what God has freely given us' (2.12), i.e. the gift of Jesus, the divine wisdom. Paul's argument proceeds until he reaches its glorious conclusion, enough to send seekers after wisdom dancing around the room in ecstasy:

> 'For who has known the mind of the Lord
> that he may instruct him?'
> But we have the mind of Christ.
> (1 Corinthians 2.16)

To summarize: the Holy Spirit who inspired and revealed the words of the New Testament 2,000 years ago receives his own words into our hearts and minds (the author is the interpreter) to release to us wisdom for living.

What are the signs, illustrations, examples and symptoms of the wisdom of the kingdom which the Spirit revealed to the Gospel writers for our instruction? We mention just three:

1 The sanctification of ordinary life[1]

There is nothing more ordinary than *the everyday act of greeting* another person in the street. In Jesus' culture exchanging greetings was an involved and significant business because a greeting was a sign of God's peace. Jesus said of the Pharisees, 'how they love to be greeted in the market-places and to have men call them "Rabbi"' (Matthew 23.7). Which one of two people meeting in the street had to give the first greeting was an issue of some importance, but Jesus swept away these conventional rules. Sophia's children 'prove her right' in her boundless grace to everyone by extending the peace of God in a greeting to everyone. No prejudice, no favouritism, no judgemental attitudes: 'And if you greet only your brothers, what are you doing more than others? Do not even pagans do that? Be perfect, therefore, as your heavenly Father is perfect' (Matthew 5.47–48).

The application of that symptom of grace may require of us a fundamental shake-up of the way we regard people (*all* people) we meet throughout the day. In our conventional, 'Hello – good morning – how are you?' greetings we will, in our hearts, wish God's peace on them. In a similar vein Jesus required of his people that they bear witness to the wisdom of the kingdom in something as simple as *self-effacing modesty*, and taking 'the lower place at the reception' (see Luke 14.7–11). In an aggressively self-promoting society we will witness to the higher wisdom of Christ's own self-emptying, and the principle of self-giving as the essence of living. A simple gesture of everyday courtesy such as standing back and holding the door open for others to pass through ahead of you is a symbolic act. You sacrifice 25 seconds of your life holding the door open, so that others can save 25 seconds of their lives. In every sphere someone must serve if others are to live. Usually we pay people for this service and don't give it a second thought, but the modest, serving-minded child of Sophia is displaying profound wisdom.

Another aspect of everyday life that reveals the divine wisdom is *our use of words*. The value Jesus placed on disciplined language is seen most disturbingly (for those of us who like to talk a lot) in the argument about what it is that 'defiles' a person. 'Listen to me, everyone, and understand this. Nothing outside a man can make him "unclean" by going into him. Rather, it is what comes out of a man that makes him "unclean"' (Mark 7.14–15). So, beware the danger of speaking unkind, thoughtless words: throwaway, jokey, insulting words, like 'Raka', meaning empty-headed, and again 'idiot', which, astonishingly, Jesus rates along with murder (Matthew 5.21)! Any words of ours that implicitly slander or spread doubts, or judge another person Jesus forbids outright. Rather, as we saw in Proverbs (see pp. 34–35) and in Paul (p. 33), our speech should be clean, tangy, encouraging, illuminating (see Matthew 5.33–37). 'Simply let your "Yes" be "Yes" and your "No", "No"; anything beyond this comes from the evil one' (Matthew 5.37). Thus the believer is called to practise unconditional truth in every area of life. Why? Because God's reign is like that.

2 *The practice of unconditional forgiveness*

This is not to practise a pretence, as though guilt is a simple thing which can be ignored. Discipline is required in the fellowship of the kingdom; wrong and harmful behaviour is confronted and dealt with (see Luke 17.3–4 where repentance is expected). But among Sophia's children the wisdom of forgiveness prevails, deriving from their own experience of boundless forgiveness and restoration at the Lord's hands. How this transforming, Christ-like attitude clears the festering rubbish from our souls, allowing us to relate to our brothers and sisters in a true simplicity of spirit. (See Chapter 8, on the generosity of the giver and the forgiver.)

3 Attitudes between men and women

Belonging to the kingdom and living within its wisdom transforms the way men and women regard each other. Jesus' own relationship with women and their attitude towards him were, in that culture, sensational. Josephus expressed the attitude typical of the time: 'A woman is in every respect of less worth than a man.'

Judaism hoped to protect women by separating them wherever possible from public gaze. The woman in the city generally kept to the house; if she went out her hair was arranged to make her virtually unrecognizable. In the light of such attitudes, the freedom with which Jesus met with women is remarkable, for instance in his declaration, 'Here are my mother and my brothers! Whoever does God's will is my brother and sister and mother' (Mark 3.34–35). Women are honoured with their rightful place in the kingdom, as a sign of the time of salvation (Joel 2.28–32, which is also quoted in Acts 2.17–21). An old rabbinic maxim says, 'Do not speak much with a woman (on the street)', but Jesus astonished and disturbed his disciples when he talked alone and openly with a woman about the deepest things in life (John 4.27). On another occasion, in a sensational encounter, a woman washed his feet with her tears, her perfume and her kisses, and dried them with her hair. Women travelled around with him and financed his mission (Mark 15.40; Luke 8.1–3), they remained unflinching in their commitment to him, to an extent far beyond the capabilities of the men, and are shown to have been light years ahead of men in grasping Jesus' meaning.

The radically new attitudes between men and women within the fellowship of the kingdom were possible because of the new expectations of personal discipline in things sexual. In the Judaism of Jesus' time the understanding was that sexual desire could not be contained, therefore the causes of temptation were removed, i.e. lock the women away. But Jesus welcomed both women and men into his company because he expected his followers to practise self-control to an astonishing degree, even within the imagination: 'Blessed are the pure in heart' (Matthew 5.8), and the great principle, 'You have heard that it was said, "Do not commit adultery." But I tell you that anyone who looks at a woman lustfully has already committed adultery with her in his heart' (Matthew 5.27–28). Where this principle is practised an authentic freedom enters into the friendship between men and women, who can live normal, relaxed 'safe' lives in relation to each other without fear of exploitation, seduction or manipulation. The application of this sign of the kingdom to our own time is too obvious and urgent to require further comment. Within Christ's wisdom men and women receive the respect and appreciation that is their due. In a society such as ours, with its universally eroticized culture (I recently heard a speaker on the radio use the phrase 'the obscene-ification of life'), the mutual consideration, valuing and protecting between men and women within Christ's discipline is surely one of the kingdom's most striking signs. Paul had our Lord's teaching concerning men and women in mind when he coined his own startling and radical maxim: 'There is neither male nor female, for you are all one in Christ Jesus' (Galatians 3.28).

Leaving aside other aspects of the 'sanctification of everyday life', including attitudes to children, work, money and the renunciation of belongings, we must refer to what is the fundamental difference between the old law and Jesus' revelation, and that is *motive.* The law of the kingdom is not merely the old, sharpened up and raised to a higher level, it is energized by the wholly different motive of an overwhelming grateful love. It is gratitude for God's love and grace in Christ. For an example, illustration, symptom of the wholly new experience of a wholly different sort of love, look at the two men who found treasure hidden in the field and the 'pearl of great price' (Matthew 13.44–46). The point of the parable is in the responses of these two vastly different sorts of men – farm labourer and antiques collector. Both were bowled over by what they found and 'in his joy' possessed it.

Given that motive, the study and practice of Christ's wisdom becomes a joyful, adventurous, inventive way of living.

Taking it further

1 Which of the various aspects of Jesus' teaching mentioned in this chapter refer most immediately to your own life?
2 To what extent are secular, media-driven attitudes towards relations between men and women infiltrating the lives of our churches? More specifically, is the manner in which men and women regard each other in your own church a clear sign of God's wisdom?
3 A task for the next 24 hours: Set yourself to wish (in your heart!) God's peace on each person you say 'Hello' to.

CHAPTER 16

The Wisdom of Sanctification

Our instinct is to tackle the Christian life rather as we would set about painting the bathroom, but before long we encounter a certain disillusionment (with our Christian life if not with the bathroom) because of the wide daylight between Christ's new expectations of us and our ability to deliver. We have unfinished business left over from the previous chapter.

It seems that the wisdom of the cross redeems from the 'curse of the law', cancelling the damning IOU (see p. 88), only to lay even greater requirements on us once we enter the kingdom of God. Realistically, who can claim mastery over every glance and thought? And who can avoid occasionally 'murdering' a neighbour with a little careless talk? The bar is set very high in the life of the kingdom; the weight of Jesus' expectations threatens to crush all joyful spontaneity out of us, if every thought and the slightest action are to be scrutinized by the CCTV camera of conscience. 'Perfection' is a tough calling, but there the command stands: 'Be perfect, therefore, as your heavenly Father is perfect' (Matthew 5.48). We wonder about the wisdom of delivering people from the tyranny of the old law, only to leave them defeated by a new one, and we are ready to hear from Jesus about his 'wisdom of sanctification' and the way holiness happens.

First, an important distinction: the old law demands what it can never give. It demands holiness, love, service, worship, but cannot lift a finger to help us achieve them. The essence of Jesus' gospel is that *he gives whatever he requires of us*; his commands are in fact promises. You may know the true story of the professional thief in Tokyo who came to faith in Christ and on his first Sunday as a Christian attended church. For the first time in his life he saw the Ten Commandments, displayed on the church wall, and was particularly intrigued by the one that said, 'You shall not steal'. Without any prompting from his new Christian friends he intuitively read it not as a grim prohibition but as a wonderful promise of new possibilities: 'Guess what! From now on you won't steal.' He had hit upon the first step in Christ's wisdom of sanctification – by grace the commands become promises.

Jesus stunned his followers with what is surely the most daunting of his expectations, 'You are the light of the world' (Matthew 5.14). We hear that pronouncement and cringe, conscious of our spiritual inadequacies and fickleness. On a particularly good day we might attain the candlepower of a 15-watt bulb, but to be called 'the light of the world' is frankly embarrassing. Therefore in the same breath Jesus proceeded to tell them how the impossible standard becomes reality; the secret is that it doesn't depend on us. He said, 'You are the light of he world. *A city on a hill cannot be hidden.*' Many of us have taken those additional words to amplify the first part of the statement: because you are the light of the world, be unafraid to witness boldly for Christ wherever you are, be seen, be known, like a city on a hill. But in that case, how could Jesus say about that city that it *cannot* be hidden, when as we know very well, our witness is all too easily hidden from sight.

Jesus is not speaking about any city, on any hill. His unmissable city on his unshakeable hill is nothing of our doing; they were here when you and I appeared on the scene and they will continue long after we have gone. *It is the city and the mountain glimpsed by the great visionary prophets, symbolizing God's presence, his purposes, his mission and his movement among the nations.*[1] It is the city of God established on the world mountain. Isaiah (740–700 BC) described it:

> In the last days
> the mountain of the LORD's Temple
>   will be established
> as chief among the mountains;
> it will be raised above the hills,
> and all nations will stream to it.

Many peoples will come and say,
'Come, let us go up to the mountain
of the LORD,
to the house of the God of Jacob.
He will teach us his ways,
so that we may walk in his paths.'
The law will go out from Zion,
the word of the LORD from Jerusalem.
(Isaiah 2.1–3)

The point is that the city and the mountain are all God's doing. The prophets picture a cataclysmic geological upheaval as an image of God's sovereign rule, which requires a total redrawing of the world's mountain-maps in which the height of a mountain signifies spiritual powers. The Himalayas sink to little more than the Pennines, while Salisbury Plain is thrust up among the greatest of the mountains. The new 'Everest' of the spiritual domain is 'the mountain of the LORD', and on its summit is the great city of God: light streams from it to the nations who are drawn towards it. The theme of the peoples of the world on pilgrimage to the city of God on the world mountain runs throughout scripture (notice Jesus' joy when Greeks come looking for him in John 12.20–24), to fulfilment in Revelation, where 'The nations will walk by its light, and the kings of the earth will bring their splendour into it' (Revelation 21.24).

Sophia's children are citizens of the city of God. Standing within its light and activity it is inconceivable that we will not share in its illumination. And because the mountain of God's sovereignty is unassailable and unshakeable by assault or earthquake our lives, too, take on that quality of constancy and permanence. What is true of the city of God's established purposes in the world enfolds also God's people. Mountain and city symbolize the way Christ gives to us what he requires of us. The key idea in 'the wisdom of sanctification' is *participation.* We do not originate light or love or holiness; rather by the Holy Spirit we joyfully participate in those blessings already established among us by God.

Next, the wisdom of sanctification takes an incredible turn. In Paul's words: 'It is because of him [God] that you are in Christ Jesus, who has become for us wisdom from God – that is, our righteousness, holiness and redemption' (1 Corinthians 1.30). It is something of a minor miracle that we could have come so far without delving into this verse, for if there is a centre-of-gravity for our subject it must be in these words. Christ Jesus, our 'wisdom', is not a divine guru-figure expounding the three essentials for communion with God (righteousness, holiness and redemption) for his followers to emulate. Rather he *became*, *fulfilled* and *achieved* them, in our place and on our behalf, as much as he achieved forgiveness of sins on our behalf.

Christ is our *righteousness*. The word means both to have a right standing with God and also the ethical quality of life consistent with that status. Our verse is saying that Christ doesn't merely point the way towards 'righteous' behaviour, he confers his righteousness on us before we have taken a step down that road. And Christ is our *holiness*, which also has two aspects. First there is the holiness of being set apart for God, an act of consecration whereby a life is wholly given over to God against all rival claims. Second, holiness is the practical transformation of a life that is best summed up in the phrase, 'the imitation of Christ'.

As with righteousness, so with holiness, Jesus Christ has lived and fulfilled all holiness on our behalf. Therefore, in our pursuit of practical holiness, in our desire to conform more and more to Christ's image, we start out from the fact that he has already gifted the holy achievement of his life to us. And he is our *redemption*. Its fundamental idea is of a liberation purchased for us by a 'redeemer' from enslavement to the power of sin and guilt. In the Old Testament, physical and social redemption was the work of a relative called in Hebrew the *Go'el*. The Go'el was honour-bound by blood ties to come to the rescue of family members in trouble. He made his family's debts and problems his own responsibility. Jesus is our Go'el. A useful exercise is to list those things in your life that hold you back from fulfilling your calling as a child of God, and then to match that list against Christ's qualities and promises as your Go'el brother. It is in the Go'el's job description to deliver his people from the power of whatever it is that enslaves them. In particular, set yourself to look into the key Go'el passage, Hebrews 2.9–18; notice there the guarantee of Jesus' solidarity and identification with his family. 'Both the one who makes men holy and those who are made holy are of the same family. So Jesus is not ashamed to call them brothers' (Hebrews 2.11).

Any list of our weaknesses can doubtless be summarized in the frank acknowledgement that 'I cannot deliver'. Measured against God's reasonable expectations as our loving Creator-Father, who of us isn't sharply conscious of the cold shadow of failure cast across our lives? Here we must allow our Go'el brother to do for us what he longs to do, which is to credit us with his achievement in place of our failure. This incredible transaction is expressed perfectly in our verse by a small preposition: 'you are *in* Christ Jesus' (1 Corinthians 1.30). Whatever Jesus is ('in whom are hidden all the treasures of wisdom and knowledge', Colossians 2.3) covers us like the clothes we wear. The New Testament also speaks of us coming to the Father '*through*' Jesus, like entering through a door; yet we leave a door behind once we have passed through it and move on, but we continue '*in*' the clothes we put on. Therefore 'in Christ' can only mean that when the Father looks at us he sees Jesus, and our standing before God is (dare we say the words?) as Christ! Gerard Manley Hopkins wrote that the person who is 'in Christ' 'acts in God's eye what in God's eye he is – Christ'.[2]

The astounding implication of this truth is that the response we should make to God (but do not because frankly we cannot, hence the cold shadow of failure chilling the soul), Jesus our saving Go'el brother has made for us. The life of love, worship and service that he offered to the Father now extends to cover us. He *is* our response to God. In faith, our response is to the response he has already made on our behalf, in our name and as us. We now live within the power and grace of all that he is and has achieved as a man. He is our perfection, by which we are released from the futile tyranny of trying to cobble together our own perfection, free now to pursue joyfully the life God has set us to live. 'Jesus Christ is our inseparable life' (Ignatius).

For an instance of Christ as our 'wisdom of sanctification', consider how he comes to the rescue of our defective prayer and worship. Imagine arriving at church on a Sunday morning for a service starting at 10 a.m. What was happening in your church at 5 a.m.? Nothing – the congregation and choir hadn't arrived, the church wasn't open, it was empty, all was quiet. Come back in five hours' time, you say, when the service starts, then the church will be filled with singing, praying, preaching. But if that is the case, then worship is something the *congregation* produces, and presumably without the congregation there is no worship. In which case, no wonder prayer and worship are so often a disappointment, for we know in our hearts that our offerings are deeply flawed, compromised, lazy, egotistical and hypocritical. If ever we needed redeeming it is in our worship and prayer.

The truth about your church on a Sunday morning is this: before you ever arrive to 'start' worship, the man Jesus (Luther called him the Proper Man) had been standing in the church all night offering true praise and intercessions to the Father. At last there *is* a man who worships with the totality of his personality, with all his love and all his mind (as each of us should but never do). He is our Go'el brother, the representative man, able to save our prayer and worship from the poor, feeble things they are by adding his praying heart and voice to ours. Thus we 'begin' worship by entering into his perfect, ceaseless worship, our minds and voices mixing with Christ's, ascending to the Father. The Holy Spirit moves between Christ and his people to co-ordinate our words with his as his perfect offering opens up to take in ours and lift it up on his and *as* his. Thus our Go'el redeems our worship and we can have full confidence that we are heard and answered when we pray and praise in Christ. The key word in this relationship is 'participation'; our worship participates in Christ's. The wisdom of sanctification lies in the truth that 'the one who makes men holy and those who are made holy are of the same family' (Hebrews 2.11).

What, then, should be our first concern on entering church for worship on a Sunday morning? It is to listen for the songs, prayers and intercessions that our brother is offering. We are taken into his worship as the Spirit inspires and directs. In summary, the 'wisdom of sanctification' is to live by the Spirit in continuous participation '*in Christ*', who covers every aspect of our existence before God.

Taking it further

Clearly there are principles to be practised:

1 Last thing at night, open your Bible at 1 Corinthians 1.30 and leave it ready at your bedside. First thing in the morning read the foundational truth about yourself as 'in Christ Jesus', his wisdom, righteousness, holiness and redemption.
2 Reflect on what it means to start the day already accepted by God 'in Christ'. Why the spiritual stress, the anxiety, the uncertainty, when your life is 'covered' by all that Christ is and has achieved?
3 And ask yourself another question: how does it affect your attitudes to know that Jesus, your Go'el brother, is already up ahead of you in the affairs of the day, fighting your battles as required by his job description?

CHAPTER 17

Be Wise Money-Changers

A parable launched these reflections on what it means to be Wisdom's children who 'prove her right' before a critical world, and we conclude with a parable. Nothing was more typical of Jesus than his favoured way of teaching, by parable and metaphor. By symbolic speech, using natural things to convey the supernatural, he cast the net of his wisdom over people's minds. A parable as Jesus used it is like a heat-proof glass placed around the flame of revelation so that a seeker may come close to ponder eternal things without being scorched:

> 'I will open my mouth in parables,
> I will utter things hidden since the creation of the
> world.'
>
> (Matthew 13.35)

When asked 'why parables?' Jesus responded with yet more. In Matthew's arrangement seven parables appear in close convoy, which is enough to challenge the liveliest imagination (Matthew 13.1–50). By the seventh the reader is like someone gasping for a drink of cold water from a plain glass after an evening of exotic cocktails. Needing respite from so much 'gradual dazzle' (see Chapter 6) we look for a straightforward, unambiguous explanation, as in 'two-plus-two-make-four'. But no, Jesus draws his parable-fest to its conclusion and application with one further parable no less teasing than the others:

> 'Have you understood all these things?' Jesus asked.
> 'Yes,' they replied.
> He said to them, 'Therefore any teacher of the law who has been instructed about the kingdom of heaven is like the

owner of a house who brings out of his storeroom new treasures as well as old.'

(Matthew 13.51–52)

The picture of Wisdom's children made wealthy (look at the content of their storeroom) through 'understanding' her teaching runs like a connecting spine through the book:

> Blessed is the man who finds wisdom,
> the man who gains understanding,
> for she is more profitable than silver
> and yields better returns than gold.
> She is more precious than rubies;
> nothing you desire can compare with her.
>
> (Proverbs 3.13–15)

And when Jesus speaks of a treasure-filled house we cannot but make the connection between it and Wisdom's great house with its seven pillars and rich hospitality (see Chapter 3 on Proverbs 9). He spoke also about another sort of house, a symbol of a condition which is money-rich but God-poor, the person who 'stores up things for himself but is not rich towards God' (Luke 12.21). Here, then, is another definition of Wisdom's effect on the mind of those who seek her. She teaches her children to read the real value of things.

A popular saying in the early Church exhorted Christians to 'be wise money-changers',[1] able to tell at a glance and by the feel of a coin if it be sound and genuine, or counterfeit. We need to be discerning enough to distinguish what is of God and what is of the other sort; what builds life and what subverts it. At a time when the clamour is for uncritical acceptance of whatever views knock on the door, for 'inclusiveness' at all costs, and, in the name of 'Christian love', the assimilation to virtually any lifestyle, the image of the Christian as the 'wise money-changer' is interesting and timely.

It suggests that the Christian's role in the life of society is to be discerning about the 'coinage' in circulation, unafraid to step outside the consensus in giving a judgement (we expect as much of our local bank manager). We are saying that Wisdom's children 'prove her right' in knowing the name and the value of things. It is as though a mad person had broken into a shop in the night and changed all the price tags around; the truly valuable now goes for a song, rubbish will cost you thousands. Strangely, the public come into the shop as if nothing unusual has happened; the fantasy will continue until some wise money-changer blows the whistle.

For an example, which makes the point well, consider the debasement of something of immense value to society, the use of Sunday. Clearly the prevailing attitude towards Sunday is that it is entirely up to each person to use it as they wish, and 'Thank heaven we are free from the gloomy interference of the Lord's Day Observance Society!' The wise money-changer will scrutinize the new Sunday 'coin' and judge that it has been drastically tampered with, devalued to near worthlessness. Two features of the original coin have been erased, scratched off by an impatient, shallow materialism. The first is that God gave the Sabbath as a priceless gift to symbolize a two-fold completion: the Sabbath celebrates the successful completion of God's work of creation (Genesis 2.1–2) and the completion of the Exodus (Deuteronomy 5.15). By resting from work once a week Israel bore unique testimony to the surrounding nations that man does not live by his own ceaseless efforts, but rests in God's providential and saving activity. How much more so when Exodus-redemption is raised to its highest power in the resurrection of Jesus Christ and Saturday-Sabbath is moved to Sunday, the first day of the week, the day of resurrection.

More than just a day off, Sunday is a weekly statement of the fundamental reality that we flourish by dependence on our Father-God, Creator and Saviour. Our Sundays are prophetic enactments of Creation's Sunday: 'There remains, then, a Sabbath-rest for the people of God; for anyone who enters God's rest also rests from his own work, just as God did from his' (Hebrews 4.9–10). But we are being drawn by cultural change into unbridled restlessness, undue zeal, greed for experience and sensation, and our Sundays are hitched to the secular wagon. How can we cope with it? By acting the 'wise money-changer', unafraid to tell the truth about materialism's damage to Sunday's beautiful 'coin'. By reclaiming the joy of Sunday, with its recreation of mind, body and spirit, its opportunities for worship and the refreshment of faith under God's word. But above all things *joy* is the atmosphere of true Sundays, anticipating the great joy to come, which Dante saw in his vision and described as, 'I saw the universe smiling.'

The value and meaning of Sunday is just one instance of how the wise money-changer evaluates life. Others include work, government, money, sex, marriage and family – in fact all the fundamentals of our existence. Why else has God placed your church where it is if not to do the work of the wise money-changer?

In Jesus' parable, 'understanding' his teaching confers wealth on Wisdom's children. This connection is powerfully expressed in Paul's words to the Colossian church: 'that they may have the full riches of complete understanding, in order that they may know the mystery of God, namely, Christ, in whom are hidden all the treasures of wisdom and knowledge' (Colossians 2.2–3). 'Understanding' discloses itself to the heart, hence the wisdom writer's intense directions:

> My son, give me your heart . . .
> Above all else, guard your heart,
> for it is the wellspring of life.
> (Proverbs 23.26; 4.23)

'Understanding' occurs in the heart, but how does it occur? By the illuminating activity of the Holy Spirit, but how does he illuminate the heart? Once more we enquire after Jesus' own experience of illumination as a man, believing that he submitted his mind to the ways of meditation taught by Israel's wisdom masters. Their teaching is 'what he filled his mind with, it is the soil in which his thoughts grew' (see p. 6). Did he memorize, 'know by heart', the astonishing love song for God's word which is Psalm 119?

> I have hidden your word in my heart
> that I might not sin against you . . .
> My eyes stay open during the watches
>   of the night,
> that I may meditate on your promises.
> (Psalm 119.11, 148)

These words are typical articulations of the individual's part in the process of 'understanding'. A variety of methods of meditation are in vogue among us today but Jesus, true to the vision of Psalm 119, made the seeking of God's mind in his revealed word the test of love for him: 'If you love me, you will obey what I command . . . If anyone loves me, he will obey my teaching. My Father will love him, and we will come to him and make our home with him' (John 14.15, 23).

By meditation on Christ's word we are put in touch with its essence. Meditation is the unhurried mulling over of a text, the walking around inside a text – quite different from the usual smash-and-grab approach of breaking it down into parts for analysis. Analysis certainly does have its place in our study of scripture (we need to know the meanings of words, etc.) but we should keep in mind Emily Dickinson's wise principle that it is a mistake to 'cut open the skylark to get at the song'. Allow the text to sing to you. Indeed Yeats called on the 'sages standing in God's holy fire' to come and 'be the singing masters of my soul',[2] which is a lovely image of meditation.

I have used elsewhere the analogy of meditation as a jeweller's polishing drum.[3] The jeweller places into the horizontal drum the stones to be polished, along with a fine carborundum paste. The drum is switched on and left to trundle around slowly for hours. The action of the stones rubbing against each other as they turn through the grinding paste smooths and polishes them, transforming dull, unremarkable stones into beautiful and interesting ones. The jeweller trusts the process. In this analogy the stones are our thoughts and the polishing paste is scripture. It is our thoughts (not scripture!) that are shaped and polished, to emerge eventually as original insights into the meanings of Christ's words, glowing like polished moonstones.

Coleridge gives another striking image of the process of meditation: 'It is not enough that we have once swallowed it [the text], the *heart* should have *fed* upon the *truth*, as insects on a leaf – till it be tinged with the colour, and show its food in every minutest fibre.' He goes on to say that our aim should be to meditate on the text, 'that sometime or other it may become your feelings'. And again, 'knowledge becomes habitual and intuitive, combines with habitual feelings'.[4] By meditation we learn to feel our thoughts and think with our hearts.

This way leads to 'understanding' which, said Jesus in his parable, makes you wealthy in a very particular sense. You have a storeroom full of treasures, old and new. Not old-fashioned and modern, but eternal truths in fresh expressions. Colossians 2.2–3 has already defined the treasures as 'Christ, in whom are hidden all the treasures of wisdom and knowledge'. And this store isn't given us for our own use exclusively. To have it and to know it is to be enriched beyond telling, but we hold it on behalf of others. The picture then is of people calling at our front door. We talk with them and gain an idea of what it is they are searching for. Going to the back of the house we select from the treasure room the particular thing from Jesus which seems to answer to our friend's search.

This picture presupposes two things: first, that we have an intimate knowledge of the treasures in our keeping, a knowledge developed through time spent in the storeroom delighting in our hoard, and second, that we look at people with the eye of a dealer: 'I have just the thing you're looking for.' We need both a knowledge of the treasure and a knowledge of the mind of the treasure-hunter. When the wise money-changer deals wisely in the riches of our Lord Jesus Christ, 'wisdom is proved right by all her children'.

Taking it further

1 List the different groups of people you relate to, such as family, workplace, leisure, neighbours and so on.
2 Under each heading jot down the names of individuals with whom you long to share your faith.

3 From your knowledge of each person in turn complete this sentence: When I think of 'John', the thing I most want him to understand about Jesus is ________.
4 Pray for opportunities to 'bring out of your storeroom' Christ's treasures to match the needs of your friends. Ask, is this how your church sees its relationship with its neighbour?

References

Chapter 1 Sophia's Children

1 Austin Farrer, *Interpretation and Belief*, SPCK, 1976, pp. 12–13.

2 T. S. Eliot, 'The Rock', *Collected Poems 1909–1962*, Faber and Faber, 1974. Used by permission of Faber and Faber Ltd.

Chapter 2 Wisdom's Charms

1 W. B. Yeats, 'The Stare's nest by my window', *Selected Poetry*, Penguin, 1991.

2 S. T. Coleridge, from his *Coleridge's Notebooks: A Selection*, ed. Seamus Perry, Oxford University Press, 2002, p. 6, n. 49.

Chapter 3 In Wisdom's House

1 John Finney, *Recovering the Past: Celtic and Roman Mission*, Darton, Longman and Todd, 1996, p. 66.

2 Don Marquis, *Archy and Mehitabel*, Faber and Faber, 1934, 'The Lesson of the Moth', p. 87.

3 Austin Farrer, *A Celebration of Faith*, Hodder, 1970, p. 165. Reprinted by permission of Hodder Arnold.

Chapter 4 Wisdom on Time

1 Hans Urs von Balthasar, *The Grain of Wheat: Aphorisms*, Ignatius Press, 1995, p. 43.

Chapter 5 Sophia and the Snake Charmer's Fee

1 Gerhard von Rad, *Wisdom in Israel*, SCM Press, 1975, pp. 24, 26.

2 G. B. Caird, *New Testament Theology*, Clarendon Press, 1995, p. 417.

3 C. F. D. Moule, ed., *Cambridge Greek Testament Commentary: The Epistles to the Colossians and Philemon*, Cambridge University Press, 1962.

Chapter 6 To Dazzle Gradually

1 W. B. Yeats, 'A Prayer for Old Age', *Selected Poetry*, Penguin, 1991.

2 Emily Dickinson, 'Poem 1129', *The Complete Poems of Emily Dickinson*, ed. Thomas H. Johnson, Faber and Faber, 1977.
3 Gerard Manley Hopkins, 'The Wreck of the Deutschland', v. 10.

Chapter 7 Along the Plateau

1 Judah Helevi (twelfth-century Jewish poet), from his poem 'The True Vision'.
2 A. Cohen, in his introduction to Ecclesiastes in *The Soncino Books of the Bible*, Bloch Publishing Company.
3 George Herbert, from his poem-hymn, 'King of Glory, King of Peace'.

Chapter 8 Expanding the Soul-Space

1 G. Bernanos, quoted by Hans von Urs Balthasar in *Man in History: A Theological Study*, Sheed & Ward, 1982, p. 267.
2 Hans Urs von Balthasar, *Aphorisms*, Ignatius Press, 1995, p. 92.
3 Quoted in Gordon S. Jackson, *Quotes for the Journey*, NavPress, 2000, p. 58.

Chapter 9 Sophia and the 'Continual Feast'

1 *The Faber Book of Aphorisms: A Personal Selection*, ed. W. H. Auden and Louis Kronenberger, Faber and Faber, 1962.
2 William McKane, *Proverbs*, SCM Press, 1970.
3 S. T. Coleridge, *Notebooks*, p. 22, n. 156.
4 W. B. Yeats, from 'Sailing to Byzantium' in *Selected Poetry*, Penguin, 1991.
5 Henry Nouwen, *Making All Things New*, Harper & Row, 1981, pp. 23–24.

Chapter 10 The Vivacious Playmate

1 William McKane, *Proverbs*.
2 Thomas Howard, *Chance or the Dance: A Critique of Modern Secularism*, Ignatius Press, 1989, p. 17.
3 Ephrem, quoted in *The Harp of the Spirit*, Fellowship of St Alban and St Sergius, 1983, pp. 10–11.
4 S. T. Coleridge, from 'The Destiny of Nations'.
5 Emily Dickinson, 'Poem 685'.

Chapter 11 Ask the Loveliness

1 Augustine, from sermon 241, ii, 2.
2 G. K. Chesterton, 'Francis' in *Twelve Types*, London, 1906.
3 Quoted in Jackson, *Quotes for the Journey*, p. 178.

Chapter 12 Kingdom Wisdom

1 G. K. Chesterton, 'Francis' in *Twelve Types.*

Chapter 13 The Wisdom of the Cross

1 C. F. Harrold, ed., *A Newman Treasury: Aphoristic Selections*, Arlington House, 1975.
2 Martin Hengel, *Crucifixion*, Fortress Press, 1978, p. 19.
3 H. Schieler, *Principalities and Power in the New Testament*, Herder, 1966, p. 28.

Chapter 14 The Wisdom of Following

1 J. Jeremias, *New Testament Theology*, SCM Press, 1975, p. 242.
2 J. Jeremias, *New Testament Theology*, p. 242.
3 George Herbert, 'Obedience', v. 4.
4 Walter de la Mare in his introduction to Edward Thomas, *Collected Poems*, Faber and Faber, 1990, p. 10.
5 Seventeenth century, translated by Edward Caswall (1817–78).
6 Mugron, Abbot of Iona (died 981), translated from the Gaelic by Thomas Owen Clancy.
7 Robert Bridges (1844–1930), based on Johann Heermann (1585–1647).

Chapter 15 The Spirit of Wisdom

1 J. Jeremias, *New Testament Theology*, pp. 219–30.

Chapter 16 The Wisdom of Sanctification

1 J. Jeremias, *The Parables of Jesus*, SCM Press, 1975, p. 217.
2 Gerard Manley Hopkins, from 'As kingfishers catch fire'.

Chapter 17 Be Wise Money-Changers

1 J. Jeremias, *The Parables of Jesus*, p. 217.
2 W. B. Yeats, 'Sailing to Byzantium', *Selected Poetry*, Penguin, 1991.
3 Dennis Lennon, *The Eyes of the Heart*, SPCK, 2000, p. 69.
4 S. T. Coleridge, *Notebooks*, p. 166, n. 156.